THE CURIOUS MIND OF
THE BUSINESS OWNER

THE CURIOUS MIND OF THE BUSINESS OWNER

HOW STRATEGIC CURIOSITY PROMOTES FINANCIAL WELL-BEING

CHRIS ARREDONDO

NEW DEGREE PRESS

THE CURIOUS MIND OF THE BUSINESS OWNER

How Strategic Curiosity Promotes Financial Well-Being

ISBN   978-1-63676-953-0   *Paperback*

978-1-63730-019-0   *Kindle Ebook*

978-1-63730-121-0   *Ebook*

I dedicate this book to four women who have influenced my life. I can never pay you back for the sacrifices and support you've given me.

To my grandma, my wife, my mother, and my little sister.

CONTENTS

———

But I, being poor, have only my dreams; I have spread my dreams under your feet; Tread softly because you tread on my dreams...

W. B. YEATS, "HE WISHES FOR THE CLOTHS OF HEAVEN"

INTRODUCTION

———

"Curiosity is one of the most valuable characteristics one can possess. When coupled with fearlessness and determination, that's freedom."

ANONYMOUS

Business ownership has been the road map to the American dream for centuries, so why are business owners struggling to keep their businesses open? Often, it's because of the principles of change. We have replaced our need for knowledge for the conveniences of life. In return, the restlessness of business ownership overcomes our good senses—causing the quality of small businesses to decline over time, influencing their closure by the tenth year. Why are small business owners misplacing their hunger for curiosity toward every aspect of their business?

I started my career as an accountant, which helped me toward my advancement as a small business consultant. I've been able to observe during this time why business owners succeed in their business ventures and why others fail. The influence these owners had on me led me to gather evidence from empirical research to help me explore and answer what the differences and similarities between small business owners, their business practices, and their personal lives were and how those differences either led to a more successfully ran business or unfortunately led to their failure.

When I decided to write this book, I knew I wanted to make the case that developing a curious mindset nurtures and therefore leads to the discipline needed for better decision-making to prevent financial failures in business, and more specifically, small business ownership. I've been exploring this connection since the decline of my own father's business, which I witnessed as an adolescent growing up. There is a recognizable yet drastically ignored relationship between emotional awareness and financial literacy of the business owner and its impact on the success of their business.

Charlie Munger, investor, former real estate attorney, and business partner to Warren Buffet, once said, "If economics is not behavioral, then what the hell is it?"[1] This statement, after giving a slight chuckle, then aroused my thought as to wonder why indeed so little is taught on financial education.

My mom would tell you I've always been a curious person and as a kid. I would write to people I admired and found fascinating, from priests to popular businesses that would show on TV in a commercial or a magazine.

---

1   BuffettMungerWisdom, "The Psychology of Human Misjudgment— Charlie Munger Full Speech," January 13, 2013, video, 2:04.

I would send letters about myself in hopes I would get a response from anyone. I would draw cartoon characters and send them to Disney as much, and I would pray for their feedback.

This curiosity would be the foundation for many of my achievements and the realization and recovery to understanding my self-doubt.

A continuous desire to learn builds stronger decision-making through building a practice of self-control. This self-control is then absorbed into our business performance. For business owners who do not practice self-control, they experience an internal conflict which in turn reflects into their business patterns. During my research, I found a study from the blog of Ness Labs which sampled 280,000 people and found the benefits to curiosity are:

1. Curiosity keeps you young if you're looking for another way to find eternal youth.
2. Curiosity helps you learn. If you're forgetful, this can help your memorization.
3. Curiosity fosters better relationships. If you're looking for deeper meaningful relationships.[2]

These benefits aid in the development of our emotional intelligence to work with the brain to create more effective measurements to run our business. Through curiosity, these measurements are created by new interpretations of new

---

2   Anne-Laure Le Cunff, "The science of curiosity: why we keep asking 'why,'" Ness Labs, accessed August 10, 2020.

information, and if incorporated into your daily routine, you can build a business that collects data both internally within your business and outside of the company to better prepare the decision-makers of the company.

Especially if you're a solopreneur, you live by the quote of former chief solutions officer, leadership coach, and best-selling author Tim Sanders from Yahoo, who states, "Your network is your net worth."[3] The more qualified people we surround ourselves with, the more dependable the information is, and more qualified information helps us make more profitable decisions for the business.

When we build an inquisitive mind from our curiosity, we can explore more stable emotions to belong to instead of dealing with the ones forced upon us. When we control our daily improvement, we lose the doubts and anxieties that take over when we are not prepared.

One of the crumbs to the curiosity pie is self-reflection. Self-reflection leads to a better recognition of our personal choices and provides us with a clearer picture of our habits and, more importantly for small business owners, our financial habits. Self-reflection guides us to the answers we need, and I feel the most beneficial approach to finding the right financial habits is to create them detached from our emotional desires.

---

3   Tim Sanders, "Put your network to good use," Tim Sanders Blog, June 9, 2009. accessed December 12, 2020.

When we examine our perceptions, we can see more clear perspectives because we are looking for an outcome free from preconditioned opinions. This concept is most important for small business owners to realize because business decisions are so closely tied to personal priorities, which differs from the corporate business perspective. Most business books on the shelves today are written aimed at corporate business.

Curiosity fosters a committed view in understanding the intangibles of business and discerning which principles are most important by strengthening relationships, finding better solution making to difficulties, and providing a greater return on acquired knowledge over time.

Nancy H. Leonard, associate professor of management at the College of Business & Economics at West Virginia University, and Michael Harvey from the University of Mississippi examined the relationship between curiosity and emotional intelligence in a sample of graduate and undergraduate students in business administration courses. The results indicate there is a significant relationship between trait curiosity and emotional intelligence. They continued by saying curiosity [has been] conceptualized as a positive emotional-motivation system associated with the recognition, pursuit, and self-regulation of novelty and challenge.[4]

I want to provide small business owners with an alternate view on operating a business successfully. As a result of

---

4   Todd B. Kashdan, Paul Rose, and Frank D. Fincham, "Curiosity and exploration: Facilitating positive subjective experiences and personal growth opportunities," Journal *of personality assessment* 82, no. 3 (2004): 291–305.

having a father who was an entrepreneur, I have a strong fascination with exploring how we make decisions due to the attachment we have to the financial status of our business. I want to share the exploration of me finding out the relationship between why my father's business and why many small businesses like his sadly and commonly disappear. I have formed a belief that successful business owners devote more time (than those less successful) in developing their curious mindset and becoming more financially experienced and emotionally stable to adjust to the life cycles of their business.

What I didn't expect was how much of an impact the ten years my dad owned the business had in shaping my life. I wonder what would've happened to my relationship with my father if he had made time for preparing, planning, and learning more about the necessary tools to manage the business and his life. A balanced mental and financial health is essential for a business owner, and having a healthy home life, in my opinion, is one of the most important factors in the consistency.

From my point of view, our home life growing up would've been a little easier if he was more curious about contributing more time to the intangibles in life. These are areas of our lives we can't see, touch, or feel but have a significant meaning to our lives, such as our education, our values, our risk tolerance, or our passions. These intangibles create more value over time to our emotional stability and financial comprehension as a result of the evolution of our self-efficacy.

"An investment in knowledge pays the best interest."

—BENJAMIN FRANKLIN

Running a small business can be a teeter-totter of emotions if our financial decisions are not resolved with an understanding of how to use money as a tool and not as the goal.

We will explore ways to accomplish this by a commitment from the small business owner to encourage curiosity, the characteristic or intangible that develops a mindset of constant learning, such as:

- Asking Questions. The technique of listening more and talking less.
- Documenting our thoughts for the day. Preferably morning reflection and evening reflection to record daily observations.
- Reading. Gathering information from diverse points of view.
- Self-reflection. Examination of controlling our behaviors and habits.

I will demonstrate how the above variables can improve decision-making over time and how neuroscience reviews can help us understand how curiosity can actually frame our behavior into producing healthy financial habits. The same research from Ness Labs I mentioned earlier shows 2 percent of adults with a curious mindset have achieved this skill set over time.[5] Over the course of the book, I will demonstrate how curiosity can help the most important aspect of a business: a capital blueprint.

When I think of the business owner whose success can be attributed to his curious mindset, which also happens to be one of the finest capital allocators, I think of Warren Buffet. I have been fascinated with Warren Buffett since my mid-twenties. He is one of the greatest financial minds in history and believes in constant learning.

Of all the things I've seen and read about him over the years, his eagerness to learn is what inspires me the most. It has been said he is one of the most curious people of all time, and this curiosity has become his superpower.

It is mentioned he dedicates up to six hours a day reading and is quoted as saying, "That's how knowledge works. It builds up like compound interest. All of you can do it, but I guarantee not many of you will do it."[6] He knows human nature will create obstacles, and our financial position will dictate most people's decision-making.

Many people will make the excuse they don't have time to add anything extra into their day. However, the underlying benefits exceed the time and effort used. The benefit of adding even an hour a day of reflection, or study time, or time

---

5   Anne-Laure Le Cunff, "The science of curiosity: why we keep asking 'why,'" Ness Labs(blog) accessed August 10, 2020.

6   Kathleen Elkins, "Berkshire Hathaway star followed Warren Buffett's advice: Read 500 pages a day," Make it (blog), MSNBC, March 27, 2018, accessed February 27, 2021.

to learning something new is not only beneficial to our life's well-being but also beneficial to our business success.

I wanted to see if Warren Buffett's mindset as a business owner was unique or part of a larger trend we could all benefit from. He said, "The way you learn about businesses is by absorbing information about them, thinking, deciding what counts and what doesn't count, relating one thing to another. And, you know, that's the job. You can't get that by looking at a bunch of little numbers on a chart bobbing up and down about a—or reading, you know, market commentary and periodicals or anything of the sort.

That just won't do it. You've got to understand the businesses. That's where it all begins and ends.[7] We can recognize it would be smart to follow the advice of one of the richest men in the world, but his message gets lost most of the time."

A distinct attribute among the successful business owners I've worked with is a desire to know and learn about every aspect of their business. Their curious mindset is always a positive link to their financial strategies that help run their business more successfully. The drive to continuously learn is critical to their overall success. The appreciation of education and, equally as important, mental endurance improves the way we learn. As information builds over time, it allows our brain to make better decisions when faced with problems or opportunities. An effective way to accomplish this is to

---

7   "Staying Curious, Investment Masters Class," (Investment Blog), June 28, 2018, accessed October 22, 2020.

activate our curiosity by spending a little time every day on the intangibles of our life that can quantify a purpose.

How can an enjoyable interest in learning help position us for long-term success? We will examine the lessons from business owners and financial professionals to discover why an interest in the intangible aspects of an owner's personal life carries over into the business practices in the developing processes, financial strategies, and relationships with people to create a stable strategy for future success. We will discuss the benefits of cultivating curiosity techniques that will improve business performance and reinforce financial strength through the various life cycles of the business.

It is my intention to use my business experience to create a new perspective about curiosity in business by exploring the difficulties of my father's business venture through what I've learned from other business owners, interviews with professionals, and scholarly research to provide data to support my findings.

My father always says, "It was the people who took the time to teach me new things that made the experience more meaningful." I consider this as an opportunity to spread awareness of the restlessness of running a business, and I hope to make it a meaningful experience.

It is learning how to be a man, a supportive husband, and an understanding father I feel is still the hardest part of everything, but it's through the personal inspection I found an improved way of looking at business. The emotional stability and positive thinking I had to discover on my own to avoid the common generational habits.

I will explain how the benefits I experienced with my own curiosity and how it can aid in our:

- *Financial literacy and its impact on our emotional intelligence*
- *Relationship between entrepreneurial curiosity and innovation*
- *Relationship between entrepreneurial curiosity and self-efficacy*
- *Relationship between intellectual capital and our financial returns*

We will use intangibles, such as curiosity, to clarify the:

- *Decreasing usefulness of financial reporting*
- *Increasing awareness of financial literacy*
- *How it can increase tangible wealth and stability*

We will then offer an answer to how the small business environment should approach the future for small businesses with a concentration on building stability from within. It starts like anything else, with purpose. The current economic system is broken, and I think I can convince you there is already a solution to fix it. In my opinion, it can be solved through the financial framework to determine a monetary value for intangible assets. Evidence supports the idea small business owners need forward-looking measurements that restore the usefulness of financial information to support the future and gauge the business more methodically and reinforced with equitable decision-making. It will take our candid curiosity to consider a new approach to operating a small business by incentivizing the business owner to build stability, positive development over a period of time, and the preparation for uncertain times.

CHAPTER 1

BE CURIOUS

———

My dad would load the family in the car and drive us around the wealthier side of town to look at houses he hoped to get us someday. I remember sitting in the back seat of my parent's car with my sister and looking out the back window with our heads pressed up against the glass, bored out of our mind as we drove around. He was determined to someday live the lifestyle he thought they had. I think he was searching for the answer to the same question I was: *How did they do it?*

In the upcoming chapters, we will explore collectively the relationship between curiosity and financial success. It may sound bizarre at first. How can something invisible create financial security? But it is true, the benefits that come from expanding our curiosity produce more positive financial decisions. More importantly, expanding our curiosity builds a deeper sense of purpose, which leads to strengthened courage, a healthy emotional intelligence, and, consequently, positive financial self-control. Self-control has already been established as a proven attribute to financial success.

Therefore, turn curiosity into the motivator en route to positive, tangible financial results or turn something intangible into something tangible. Prepared thoughts deliver prepared actions, which transfer prepared results.

To accomplish this, we must accept responsibility for the failure of our current economic system. Milton Friedman had a big hand in it as well. This system will struggle to carry small businesses into the next era, especially if small businesses are struggling to survive now. Just look at the global impact pressures such as COVID-19 have had on our communities. Can we honestly say small business owners are prepared for new technologies, new financial tools and techniques, and an awareness in handling the crisis points in our business?

When my father eventually decided to become a business owner after fourteen years of working for Union Pacific Railroad, he recognized for him, owning his own business was the best profitable answer to a more sophisticated way of living. However, even though it took me longer to find an explanation, I learned it takes a lot more than money and determination to carry out this plan. It takes a lot of curiosity to find a "grounded confidence" to learn self-control, financial literacy, and self-awareness to build peace of mind as a business owner.

For this reason, I have always been captivated by the stories from business owners about what led them to start the journey of self-employment. I've been a fanboy of Warren Buffett and Charlie Munger, two of the most prominent investors of all-time. I may be biased, but their principles and investment strategy have proven themselves time and time again.

I've had the advantage of working and meeting with a collection of talented business owners—people from all different backgrounds and aspirations. Those differences framed their financial proficiency. My relationship with them has influenced my studying the connection between our emotions and how it affects our financial decisions. I've recognized their desires are all connected in some way, and some approach their aspirations uninformed.

During my consulting days, my preparatory meetings with clients revealed their financial philosophies. For many, it was obvious those more successful business owners recognize their principles must be aligned with personal self-control. The business owners who lack this intuition make up a large percentage of the businesses that fail every year. Curiosity is one clear influential charm successful business owners have that benefits in preserving their uniqueness and safeguarding their resources. It teaches us the meaning of our unique purpose and gives us an interest in all aspects of the business to be a better leader, a better follower, and provides overall peace of mind.

Self-control has been linked to financial success. *The Journal of Behavioral and Experimental Finance* published a recent article questioning how gathering and interpreting information influences our financial management and our overall financial success. Self-control, or the ability to resist urges and self-regulate unwanted behavioral impulses, is a key determinant of success in most areas of life.[8] This seems to be

---

8   Holly Ventura Miller, J. C. Barnes, and Kevin M. Beaver, "Self-control and health outcomes in a nationally representative sample," American *journal of health behavior* 35, no. 1 (2011): 15–27.

true also for behavior in the financial domain, but research showed that self-control predicted both sound financial behavior and financial well-being.[9]

In this study, they associated the behaviors to responsibilities of an executive in what they list as three separable but moderately correlated functions:

- Inhibition
- Working Memory
- Shifting

In the manner they have defined these functions, I use these functions to establish the relation to the responsibilities of a small business owner. Over the years of working with business owners, I feel these functions best explain the everyday expectations of a business owner from managing people, capital structure, financial management, efficient processes and procedures, bills, and the list goes on and on.

The main theme of the research continues with an interpretation of these responsibilities that self-control, a healthy mind, financial literacy, and reliable support are required for financial success.

They state, "Inhibition refers to the ability to control one's attention, behavior, thoughts, and emotions and steer them toward appropriate responses, such as continuing working

9   Camilla Strömbäck, Thérèse Lind, Kenny Skagerlund, Daniel Västfjäll, and Gustav Tinghög, "Does self-control predict financial behavior and financial well-being?" Journal of Behavioral and Experimental Finance 14 (2017): 30–38.

on a boring task instead of doing something more rewarding and pleasurable."[10]

"Thus, inhibition overlaps with many common definitions of self-control. Working memory or updating involves the ability to maintain and update information in a mental workspace, such as remembering and internally repeating a phone number. Finally, shifting refers to the ability to switch attention flexibly between goal-relevant tasks, i.e., multitasking. Thus, shifting enables individuals to change perspective when stuck on a difficult problem and to consider someone else's point of view."[11]

I've always been an avid notetaker. I take notes on just about everything you can think of, motivational videos, business interviews with CEOs, a shit load of books intertwined with the notes from conferences I attended, and business meetings I've attended for work and volunteer purposes. In the process of writing this book, I went back through some of my old journals and notebooks. The notes I enjoyed reading were from first meetings with people and projects with clients and employers.

My journals contain the counsel from people I worked for, a city project uniting two countries to help diversify my hometown, notes from my board meetings to bring the credit union to my hometown, and my emotions throughout my life. I knew I wanted to write a book about business, and I knew I wanted to write a book people could learn from. So,

---

10   Ibid
11   Ibid

I combed through the lessons and notes, and I investigated the common factors between them. I was looking for the common theme between my past experiences and the insight I've acquired over my career. What I determined was there is an apparent connection in common among the successful business owners. It is their undeniable curiosity. It is their successful habits built from continuous learning that connects them to their financial well-being.

I wanted to concentrate on helping small business owners succeed. Since most of my career has been working with small business owners by virtue of accounting, consulting, or financing, I needed to figure out what problems were preventing so many of them from success in the first place. The most common reason noted from the media is small business owners do not have adequate access to capital or credit. While lack of access to capital or credit is a substantial problem, it runs deeper than that.

I read a statement from Kimber Lanning, executive director of Local First Arizona, a small business advocate, and entrepreneur, in a recent article saying, "There is the need for smaller loans and a line of credit products that are conducive to small businesses. Bring back relationship banking where getting to know and mentoring small business owners creates a pipeline for other bank products and strengthens the local economy."[12] In agreement with Mrs. Lanning, we need to teach small business owners financial safeguards and emotional self-control.

---

12 Kimber Lanning, "Lack of Access to Capital is Crippling the US Small Business Sector in Communities of Color," Interise Connect (blog), Interise, accessed January 10, 2021.

It is hard to understand why the success rate of businesses decreases over time. I've come to believe one major contributing factor in the reason small business owners fail is due to the owner's emotional tie to the business.

When the owner lacks emotional stability, it weakens the owner's execution of their executive responsibilities. Their courage declines, and their purpose doesn't inspire them past their shortcomings. They become too vulnerable to forces beyond their control, such as competitive forces, economic forces, natural forces, even international and governmental forces.

There is an increasing level of financial instability with the business structure instead of a consistent harmony of profit and expansion. After exploring this, what I've found is distressing. As the business evolves, successful business owners transition into new processes and procedures, innovative products and services, attainable financing, and systems and controls for financial safeguards. The ones who fall victim to the serial killer of businesses—cash flow—do not. These lacks of financial controls are what gets them eliminated.

The union between a business owner's mental health is closely related to that of their financial health. Emotional research shows the deterioration of one's personal mental health inflates financial failure. So, as the business begins to decline, the emotional snowball of fear and doubt starts rolling downhill.

My dad told me as his business started to dissolve, "It was hard to talk to anyone. I was embarrassed. I felt all alone."

There wasn't anyone he felt comfortable approaching about it. Even though he felt he was alone, he wasn't alone. Many business owners struggle with this feeling of isolation. Warwick business schools Small and Medium-Sized Enterprise Centre prepared a working paper illustrating the significance of studying the effects of business failure. "Life after Business Failure: The Process and Consequences of Business Failure for Entrepreneurs" classifies "the primary costs of business failure as financial, social, and psychological."[13] We will use the consequences identified in this research alongside other studies on the financial and social, but most importantly, the psychological impact of business failure.

Few studies have explored the link between self-control and broader, more general, measures of financial behavior.[14] I have spent the last year scouring through information to support the case that curiosity can prevent business failure by promoting positive financial, social, and psychological habits that contribute to our financial success. What I discovered is curiosity enhances our learning and interpretation process that drives our mental proficiency.

A failure of any kind can be frightening for a small business owner because every financial decision has an emotional connection. As business owners, we view our business as a part of our own identity, and when our business faces a

---

13   Deniz Ucbasaran, Dean A. Shepherd, Andy Lockett, and S. John Lyon, "Life after business failure: The process and consequences of business failure for entrepreneurs," Journal *of management* 39, no. 1 (2013): 163–202.

14   Camilla Strömbäck, Thérèse Lind, Kenny Skagerlund, Daniel Västfjäll, and Gustav Tinghög, "Does self-control predict financial behavior and financial well-being? "Journal *of Behavioral and Experimental Finance* 14 (2017): 30–38.

struggle, it's hard to accept defeat. But it doesn't have to be. What successful business owners recognize is there is a purpose to financial planning, skill development, and leadership maturity.

The economic system rewards those who are prepared, analytical, and tenacious. These attributes are not granted to a select group of people. These attributes belong to everyone and can be cultivated through curiosity.

Research provided by scholarly articles on the correlation between financial literacy and firm performance, financial problems, and psychological distress, psychological determinants of entrepreneurial success, and life satisfaction, new accounting methods will set the stage for discussing a new way of creating business value. This means recording financial transactions regularly and using them to make financial decisions throughout the life of the business. Of the businesses I work with, the most successful ones utilize financial tools like financial statements or strategic metrics to help make financial decisions.

The other majority are only concerned about having their personal and business financial reporting prepared when filing taxes or are trying to obtain capital. These moments are too late to think about why problems exist in the company. The consequences are missed opportunities to use them for preparation and proper financial decision-making. A large majority of small business owners are not prepared when it comes to providing accurate, regularly collected financial data. In countless conversations with business owners who seek funding and investment for their business, many of them are not attuned to their correct financial situation.

They are managing their business by their bank account balance. The problem with that practice is they never truly understand their financial position. More importantly, by only using the bank account balance to manage the business, it causes bad financial habits by ignoring the analysis of financial ratios. Investopedia defines ratio analysis as "a quantitative method of gaining insight into a company's liquidity, operational efficiency, and profitability by studying its financial statements such as the balance sheet and income statement. Ratio analysis is a cornerstone of fundamental equity analysis."[15] The fundamental analysis measures the effects of economic and financial factors on an investment.

In a 2014 study, *The Scholar Commons Journal* for the University of South Florida published "Financial Literacy and the Success of Small Businesses: An Observation from a Small Business Development Center." In the article, they stated,

> *"When the financial literacy skills of entrepreneurs fall short of those needed to operate a successful business, it is more than the individual business at risk. Financial ratios were used to analyze the business's financial condition. While performing the financial analysis of these firms, we also surveyed the business owners to determine their level of financial understanding and their use of financial statements in making management decisions. We found a strong*

---

15 "What is Ratio Analysis?" Investopedia, accessed January 10, 2021.

association between the small businesses' financial strength and the business owners' habits of mind with regard to their financial statements: for 7/14 of the businesses, the business owner did not regularly review financial statements, and 6/7 of those businesses were experiencing financial difficulties; conversely, 7/14 of the businesses in the study were experiencing financial difficulties, and for 6/7 of them, the business owner did not regularly review the financial statements."[16]

There is a common theme continuing to reveal itself, which is successful business owners practice self-control, are financially literate, carry out financial safeguards, and manage their executive responsibilities profitably. Now you might tell yourself, "It's easier to have stability when you already have a start."

To that, I would reply, "We are all born with curiosity. We can always learn something new. That is our superpower!" For many people, I'll speak in the context of our childhood because that's where education begins. The opportunity to learn is effortless. Their parents are educated, their parents are financially stable, their parents are emotionally stable, and education becomes an acquired behavior.

On the other hand, there are many children who don't have it so easily.

---

16   Pearl Dahmen and Eileen Rodríguez, "Financial Literacy and the Success of Small Businesses: An Observation from a Small Business Development Center," Numeracy: *Advancing Education in Quantitative Literacy* 7, no. 1 (2014).

I met a young girl when I volunteered with the Hispanic Chamber of Commerce in my local city through an event for a local alternative center for at-risk kids. She was enrolled into this secondary school that specializes in students who have been removed from their original school as a disciplinary action for behavior not proper for a traditional setting.[17] She was there because she couldn't control *her home life*. Her probation officer showed up at her house for an examination, and she was arrested for being around drugs that belonged to her mother, a known drug addict. At one of the breaks, she came to the back of the room to ask me a question, and it was at that moment I realized how lost we both were.

Do you think I could get into cosmetology school?

She would take the advice from a total stranger because she didn't know if she'd have another chance to speak to someone she trusts to listen to her dreams. My advice to her now would be a little more insightful after the struggles I had after our talk, but my overall principle remains the same, we must always have a constant desire to learn more. At that time, I told her to read as many books as she could get her hands on. Curiosity is one of the only ways to challenge our environment and pursue positive, equitable, and moralistic habits. Her acquisition of knowledge was probably one of the few things in her life she could control.

For this reason, I think it is imperative we continue to learn more about curiosity, how it positively changes our cognitive

---

17   Alternative Education Center, "Mission/vision," accessed January 13, 2021.

behavior, and what it does to the brain to make better decisions, to challenge our doubts and fears, to prepare and plan for qualified financial safeguard.

CHAPTER 2

STAY CURIOUS

———

Warren Buffet says what kills great businesses is complacency. Warren says, "You want restlessness, a feeling that
someone is always after you, but you're going to stay ahead
of them."[18] Curiosity has been consistently recognized as
a critical motive that influences human behavior in both
positive and negative ways at all stages of the life cycle. It has
been identified as a driving force in child development and
as one of the most important spurs to educational attain-
ment.[19,20] This shouldn't come as a surprise when academics
found that curiosity has also been cited as a major catalyst
behind scientific discovery, possibly eclipsing the drive for
economic gain.[21]

---

18   The Coca-Cola Company, "Warren Buffett on Why He'll Never Sell a
     Share of Coke Stock," Coca-Cola 2013 Annual Shareowners meeting,
     YouTube video, :48, https://youtu.be/4p1_5bZ8I4M.

19   H.I. Day, "Curiosity and the interested explorer," Performance and
     Instruction, 21, 19–22.

20   D.N. Stern, "The interpersonal world of the child," New York: Basic Books,
     (2007).; Wohlwill, J.F., "Curiosity, imagination, and play," Hillsale, NJ,
     (pp1–21), (1987).

21   A. Koestler, "The act of creation," New York: Dell, (1973).; Simon, H. "The
     cat that curiosity couldn't kill," Working paper, Department of Psychol-
     ogy, Carnegie Mellon University, (1992).

Business owners are relentlessly trying to create a successful business, and while the lifestyle of the business owner gets romanticized in the media, especially social media, there are a large majority of business owners who fall victim to under-achievement and misfortune. According to the US Bureau of Labor Statistics, reported by Investopedia, the percentage of business closure only increases from year one to year ten.[22] Depending on where you look for this statistic, it's anywhere from 7 to 20 percent in year one and 50 to 65 percent by year ten. There are scenarios influencing these figures. For instance, if the business owner retires or the business owner closes one business to open another, that magnifies the percentages, but the overall numbers are still astonishing.

In any case, the failure rate continues to rise year over year, and it is a systemic problem. Scholars have studied this problem and what they found is discouraging. The impact of financial literacy, resource flexibility, investigating the business intangibles, and boosting curiosity have on small businesses is significant. These factors have a positive effect when the business owner is financially literate. They have easier access to capital, they understand their organizational processes, and they have a constant desire to learn.

Throughout the book, I will refer to business owners in conflicting ways when comparing success. For this reason, I want to point out I am not comparing based on a purely financial perspective. The main purpose is for the overall well-being of the entrepreneur and progressively reaching to

---

22 "Top 6 Reasons New Businesses Fail," Investopedia, accessed January 23, 2021.

the people who work and support the entrepreneurial venture in a healthy way. Not everyone's journey is the same, and not everyone gets to their success the same way.

When I reference "successful," it's to emphasize maximum effort, maximum financial harmony, and maximum personal awareness, and not in an everyday type of way but in a habitual personal effort to fight against the setbacks that surface in entrepreneurship. An unsuccessful business owner can habituate into a successful pattern.

I created a guideline for curiosity through fascinating research from scholars and interviews with small business professionals and garnished with personal experiences with entrepreneurs as an accountant, small business consultant, CFO, and investor.

One of the biggest factors of small business owner failure is the lack of financial literacy. They never learned the importance of financial statements, evaluating influential ratios, or explaining their organizational processes. These factors are a main reason many of them are not profitable and are in financial hardship. In return, these companies are teetering on the brink of closure and have no idea how or why. These unsuccessful business owners are not aware until they're able to review financial statements and reveal areas where the business is vulnerable and contributing to the lack of capital and inability for investment.

These businesses were managing their money on damaged information. One big reason is unsuccessful business owners are storing their financial decisions in their heads and the bank account at a glance. For example, the problem arises when they're caught off guard by a bill they forgot, and the check they were hoping for did not come in.

The minds of these owners were stuck in short-term problems, so they were not able to detect the negative consequences of not establishing financial protocols to transform their negative position. These business owners are not isolated in the overall confusion of small business education. So far in studies on entrepreneurship, the goal-directed behavior approach has been used, but mostly in the intention to study start-up businesses. This doesn't help those in a state of anxiety with no capital.

Why is there an increasing level of instability instead of a consistent harmony of profit and expansion?

Do we need to be prepared emotionally to deal with the lack of financial data necessary to make effective decisions?

Since broad personality traits are not directly related to business success, goal commitment was introduced as a moderating variable between psychological characteristics and entrepreneurial success.[23] This study validates that, among any other categorization of people, entrepreneurs have a stronger desire for career performance. Their behavior toward their effort runs positively alongside their business success. This can be positive or negative. I remember seeing

---

23 A. Rauch & M. Frese, "Born to be an entrepreneur?" Revising the personality approach to entrepreneurship, In J. R. Baum, M. Frese, & R. A. Baron (Eds.), *The psychology of entrepreneurship* (pp. 41–65), Mahwah: Erlbaum. (2007).

my father during times the business was booming and when it wasn't doing very well. My dad has always been known as a jokester, but during the moments, he had more business than he could handle, and he worked himself hard and was disorganized. He had a "hustle hard" mentality that believed sales would fix everything.

Aside from all the unfavorable evidence, the solution is simple. It is not hard to understand why the success rate of businesses is only 18 percent within a ten-year period, and it is not completely the psychological makeup of the business owner. Financial proficiency intertwines with emotional mastery to enhance risk awareness.

Financial decisions are shaped by financial education, and our psychological emotions can get in the way, especially during times of uncertainty. I wanted to concentrate on helping small businesses succeed, so I looked back at all my business experiences to search for the understanding I gathered over the past fifteen years.

Looking back on watching my father's business dissolve and then looking back on my opportunity of having the chance to work for one of the smartest business minds, I studied the differences. Comparing the two situations, I noticed what worked and what didn't work. More importantly, I noticed why. What I found was curiosity builds an internal strength or a "grounded confidence" that eliminates the emotional attachment to money. This is especially true when the business owner struggles with their business not performing well. We can avoid self-inflicted problems by detaching our emotions from financial decisions.

Dean A. Shepherd, the David H. Jacobs Chair in Strategic Entrepreneurship at the Kelley School of Business, studied grief to explore the emotions after business failure. He suggested the loss of a business from failure can cause the self-employed to feel grief, a negative emotional response interfering with the ability to learn from the events surrounding that loss.[24] Curiosity can set the groundwork for finding the appropriate protocols to prevent psychological distress in the middle of financial hardships.

Financial development requires expanding your knowledge of financial information for budgeting, planning, and strategizing. Financial knowledge directly correlates with self-beneficial financial behavior. It can be argued stronger financial knowledge is relevant in overcoming difficulties in accessing and managing credit markets.[25]

As the lifespan of the business continues to grow, failing business owners do not transition into new processes and procedures because they are not willing to change. These business owners, over time, lose interest in innovation and get into the habit of complacency and reactionary decision-making. Mel Scott and Richard Bruce's article "Five Stages of Growth in Small Business" in the *Long Range Planning Journal* states crises tend to be disruptive, and the problems of change can

24 Deniz Ucbasaran & Shepherd, Dean & Lockett, Andy & Lyon, John, "*Life After Business Failure: The Process and Consequences of Business Failure for Entrepreneurs*," Journal of Management. 39. 163 2002. 10.1177/0149206312457823.(2013).

25 S. Adomako, an A. Danso, "Financial Literacy and Firm performance: The moderating role of financial capital availability and resource flexibility," International Journal of Management & Organizational Studies, 3 (4).

be minimized if managers are proactive rather than reactive to change.[26]

In a 2014, *The Scholar Commons Journal* for the University of South Florida published "Financial Literacy and the Success of Small Businesses: An Observation from a Small Business Development Center." In the article, they stated,

> *"When the financial literacy skills of entrepreneurs fall short of those needed to operate a successful business, it is more than the individual business at risk. Financial ratios were used to analyze the business's financial condition. While performing the financial analysis of these firms, we also surveyed the business owners to determine their level of financial understanding and their use of financial statements in making management decisions. We found a strong association between the small businesses' financial strength and the business owners' habits of mind with regard to their financial statements: for 7/14 of the businesses, the business owner did not regularly review financial statements, and 6/7 of those businesses were experiencing financial difficulties; conversely, 7/14 of the businesses in the study were experiencing financial difficulties, and for 6/7 of them, the business owner did not regularly review the financial statements."[27]*

---

26 Mel Scott, Richard Bruce, *"Five stages of growth in small business,* Long Range Planning," Volume 20, Issue 3, 1987, Pages 45–52, ISSN 0024-6301.

27 Pearl Dahmen and Eileen Rodríguez, *"Financial Literacy and the Success of Small Businesses: An Observation from a Small Business Development Center,"* Numeracy 7, Iss. 1 (2014): Article 3.

This is also the leading explanation behind why my father's business ultimately closed. In his words, "I didn't have time to get into the office part of it, plus I trusted the staff knew how to take care of all that. I was the one doing sales, repairs, and deliveries, and after-hour repairs." Ultimately, not getting familiar with the internal functions of the office lead to loss of cash flow for the company. When the internal operations were overlooked, certain areas of the business hurt the growth.

Accounts receivables were ignored, so my father continued to work for people who owed him for months, and he never received payment. This habit is a common trend among failing business owners who do not use their accounting system properly.

Successful business owners are constantly looking for missing holes in their cash flow. They involve professionals in the planning of the business. CPAs are not only for tax preparation, and when they are only used during tax season, the business is not fully benefiting from tax strategy, filling in the gaps of financial knowledge and accountability to a plan. A good financial professional like a CPA specializes in assisting in ongoing tax planning personally, financially, and strategizing for forthcoming opportunities in the business. They are not just there to be asked, *"Can you do my taxes?"*

For instance, I spoke with Lisa Carrasco. She works with start-ups and small businesses with no more than one hundred thousand dollars in annual revenue. Her niche is restaurants, specifically food trucks. She recognizes most of the businesses she works for need help with accounting and using their accounting system properly. She observes many small business owners going through the struggles of gathering receipts, bank statements, and other documents at the end of the year. She comments, "Most of them think it's only billing and receivables."

Unsuccessful business owners are too often only concerned with gathering expenses for tax deductions but ignore the actual financial health of the business. They spend too much time thinking sales are going to fix their problems. It doesn't only happen with small businesses. I've seen it with medium to larger businesses. People don't start analyzing their problems until it's too late. However, successful business owners have the capital to work through the inefficiencies.

Those that fail go through a snowball of problems. Because of the lack of checks and balances to maximize cash, they accumulate debt to make up for the lack of cash, and they think if they hustle more, they'll get one more run and *hope* for the best.

As Lisa continues to spell out, "Most business owners I see don't want to deal with the business side of things. When I show them their financial reports and show them how to use their accounting system, I see them get overwhelmed with all the new information."

I learned from working in corporate accounting the importance of analyzing financial statements monthly to help make better decisions. The common theme in the causes of failure is also linked to the emotional balance and financial proficiency of the business owner. We will explore the factors of failure for small businesses recognized by the academic community. These studies will equip us with the evidence for understanding these influences and prevent the deterioration of failing businesses.

The influences researched in part by the Iowa Small Business Development Center and the Iowa State University Cooperative Extension will serve as variables in explaining the causes of financial impairment in business based on:

- **Entrepreneurial intensity.** (Resiliency) Characteristics and behaviors that are unique to entrepreneurs
- **Task motivation.** (Optimism) Entrepreneur's motivation to achieve goals
- **Behavioral strategic sophistication.** (Efficiency) Implementing sophisticated strategic management practices
- **Cognitive strategic sophistication.** (Hope) Comprehension of strategic management practices
- **Environmental influences.** Choices in response to environmental factors
- **Task environment factors.** Structure of the industry in which the business operates

These intangibles are influential in developing the team, creating financial guidelines, understanding business concepts, and analyzing the business consistently. It begins with an individually trained cognitive-behavioral process. Cognitive development is how we think and process information. It is how we interact with the world with our knowledge, our memory, and decision-making.

According to the Encyclopedia of Children's Health, only 35 percent of high school graduates in industrialized countries obtain formal cognitive operations.[28] Most of us, as we enter into adulthood, haven't fully developed our capability of thought processes, including remembering, problem-solving, and decision-making.

Curiosity can help fill the gap for the adults that didn't grow up in a secure and stable environment. As the Encyclopedia of Children's Health describes, when referring to parents and *any* adult responsible for a child, they can provide stimulating learning materials and experiences from an early age, read to and talk with their children, and help children explore the world around them. As children mature, parents can both challenge and support the child's talents. Although a supportive environment in early childhood provides a clear advantage for children, it is possible to make up for early losses in cognitive development if a supportive environment is provided at some later period, in contrast to early disruptions in physical development, which are often irreversible.

This can give us a head start, but if for many of us we didn't have the privilege so as we grow older, we must read often, listen to others, and slowdown in order to develop stronger decision-making skills as an adult and business owner.

As an adult, the effort to understand business procedures and implement the processes to make profitable financial decisions according to the research does not come naturally

---

28   "Cognitive Development," Encyclopedia of Children's Health, accessed May 7, 2021.

because our cognitive operations are not fully formalized by adulthood. Revealing another reason businesses fail, if we don't work on our information processing into adulthood and business ownership, how will we know how to put our ideas into action?

- *How can we plan for the future if we do not calculate and monitor the financial gauges of the business?*
- *How can we calculate and monitor the financial gauges if our reporting processes are impaired?*
- *How are we making sure the processes are working if we are not training our staff, enforcing processes, and putting in new technologies to support the management of the business?*

It is then no surprise the percentage of successful businesses over a ten-year period closely relates to the percentage of businesses that use financial reporting as a tool to manage their business. These successful companies are observing the business through key identifiers of their business to expose variables that disrupt profit and highlight unusual effects to trends. They monitor financial measurements to identify problems in the cash flow process.

There is a developing discussion that the gap between small businesses and their innovation is growing because of the lack of attention to the intangible aspects of the business. *Harvard Business Review* performed a study that showed "a significant difference between the success and failure of small firms, and the common theme is an investment in the intangibles."[29] The research expands to describe the growth opportunities for small businesses are shrinking, and the nimbleness and grit are increasingly under pressure. Smaller companies are becoming more vulnerable to external dangers, but an investment in the internal factors and the intangibles can minimize the threat of hardships.

I began my research to help show business owners how they can structure the business and how they can amplify business profits. What I found was through intangible assets, we can build our business value, and I will make the case that by adding financial value to intangible assets, we can build internal strength in our companies and build our global economy.

Over 90 percent of our global economy is made up of small businesses, but within this majority, there are many business owners who ignore the important aspects of financial understanding. The accounting industry needs to set the framework to move toward the hyper era of technology and new business models for the future. PricewaterhouseCoopers (PwC), one of the big four accounting firms, has recognized these challenges and recognizes, "Business models have evolved in the last decade to create economic value from investments in intangible assets. This intangible-centric approach has become more pronounced since the global pandemic."[30] They continue by notifying us, "Since 2009, the implied market of intangible assets at S&P 500 companies

---

29 "The Gap Between Large and Small Companies Is Growing. Why?" Harvard Business Review accessed January 14, 2021.

30 "The unbalanced balance sheet: Making intangibles count," Viewpoint(blog), PricewaterhouseCoopers, accessed February 24, 2021.

increased 255 percent, while the book value of tangible assets only increased 97 percent over the same period."[31]

I came across a book written by Baruch Lev, the Philip Bardes Professor of Accounting and Finance at New York University Stern School of Business. Professor Lev has been with NYU for over twenty years. In his interview clip with SaderTV, he was asked what the biggest factor was inversely affecting accounting usefulness. He responded by saying the accounting industry missed the change in the business models of businesses today because businesses are investing more into intangible assets, almost twice as much as they are investing in tangible assets.

He continues by saying, "It used to be that values of companies earnings, changes in assets were created by factories, by machines, by inventories, by tangible assets, things that you can touch, when they fall, they make noise. This changed and starting roughly twenty-five years ago the value creators are making intangible assets, these are patents, brands, and information systems, and very talented and trained employees and things like that."[32]

I explored more of Baruch's investigation into constructing a new system in accounting for valuing business toward the advancement into the future. Before his message gets lost, I wanted to learn as much as I could to help business owners like my father, who need to be prepared for *what's coming*. Baruch is challenging the notion that there is a widespread

---

31   Ibid
32   SaderTV, Baruch Lev.

"dissatisfaction" with financial statements, and it is corroborated by empirical evidence which consistently documents a decreasing ability of financial information and earnings to reflect enterprise performance, predicts future performance, and explain share prices and returns.

Surveys reveal many financial executives believe financial reporting has "degenerated" into an ever-more-burdensome "compliance exercise" rather than an endeavor to inform stakeholders.[33] If financial statements are missing the mark in aiding businesses to make financial decisions and small businesses are not analyzing the financial data to help with decision-making, then what chance do business owners have in beating the increased chance of failure year after year?

Baruch says, "These documents move mountains, so what happens if they're based on faulty indicators that fail to show the true value of the company? So maybe the secret is in the intangibles?" The Merriam-Webster definition of intangible is: An asset (such as goodwill) that is not corporeal, so in other words, an asset that has no physical existence. An abstract quality or an attribute. When you google intangible, you get the definition of intangible as an intangible thing, and the underlying explanation adds "intangibles like self-confidence and responsibility."[34]

I think it's safe to say we should really start hearing a debate on change for the current ways of running our business. We can all relate to the google definition in understanding how

33   SaderTV, Baruch Lev.
34   *Merriam-Webster.com Dictionary*, s.v. "intangible," accessed March 22, 2021.

important living with a positive mindset and handling our responsibilities can have in our financial success, but we tend to miss the value of intangible assets in the literal sense of something not physical in nature, such as patents, copyrights, and brand value, but more importantly the value of research and development, innovation, and incorporating a structured strategy process. It's because you can't find the financial value of these types of assets on the balance sheet, the accounting statement that provides a review of your financial position. *We'll explore why later.*

ASSETS = LIABILITIES + OWNER'S EQUITY

As defined in Investopedia, "Assets are what a company uses to operate its business, while its liabilities and equity are two sources that support these assets."[35]

Unfortunately, intangibles do not have a value in financial reporting at the moment, but we can see how important it is from an example on Investopedia. Investopedia provides an example of Coca-Cola in saying that "A business such as Coca-Cola wouldn't be nearly as successful if it were not for the money made through brand recognition. Although brand recognition is not a physical asset that can be seen or touched, it can have a meaningful impact on generating sales."[36]

---

35   "Reading the Balance Sheet," Investopedia, accessed February 27, 2021.
36   "Intangible Asset," Investopedia, accessed February 27, 2021.

Intangible assets can provide a greater net worth to the business than what is perceived by business owners. I will use research from academic journals, interviews with business owners, interviews with financial experts, and interviews with directors of respected universities and small business development centers.

The connection between intangible capital and its path to tangible capital is so important yet often overlooked. We will examine the importance of creating organizational processes, creating action items to achieve goals, and implementing checks and balances to maximize profit and initiate a specific strategic plan that can benefit small business operations.

We will explore the benefits of making "things you cannot see" a necessary part of accessing money that prevents us from starting, expanding, or purchasing a business. The influence human, social, information, and emotional capital has on financial capital is discounted because there isn't a financial value in the current model of financial reporting. Incorporating a value for these intangible aspects of the business can lead to a better valuation of businesses competing in the information age.

- *Human Capital.* Creating an environment that encourages an exchange of ideas through communication.
- *Social Capital.* Creating a network of people that hold us accountable.
- *Information Capital.* Creating processes that capture as much information as possible about the business to make informed decisions.

- *Psychological Capital.* Creating an understanding of who we are as a leader of an organization.

These areas of our businesses are often ignored because we use our past financial circumstances as a frame of reference to dictate the future of the business without evolving in ways that support financial decision-making. The business must be built on an internal foundation from business concepts, operational processes, and team development through an internal reflection of goals, strategies, and communication.

In the *PwC Viewpoint* blog titled "The unbalanced balance sheet: Making intangibles count," they state the accounting models and business valuation has not changed, and the new valuation needs to introduce a financial quality for intangible assets. This has the potential to build small business owners' understanding in the right areas necessary to build a steady, profitable business. They go on to say, "The increasing proportion of company value represented by intangible assets reflects not only greater investment, but also attributes of these assets that make a company worth more than its book value."[37]

Your business can only last a certain amount of time without incorporating proper measurement tools to manage the business. Many business owners start by diving right into the thick of things and don't take time to understand all of the internal aspects of running a business.

---

37 "The unbalanced balance sheet: Making intangibles count," Viewpoint(blog), PricewaterhouseCoopers, accessed February 24, 2021.

This contributes to another reason businesses fail. The business owners' lack of financial literacy interferes with the analysis of their financial statements.

If research provides that successful businesses are examining financial evidence, why do almost half of small businesses (45 percent) employ neither an accountant nor a bookkeeper, and still as of 2018, one-quarter of small businesses (25 percent) still record their finances on paper instead of on a computer?[38] They are only concerned about having their financial data compiled during tax season or when they are trying to secure capital. The consequences are missed opportunities to use them for financial decision-making and the inability to qualify for financial investment.

During my conversations with the directors of Bam Biz Hub, a nonprofit that focuses on educating small business owners, the president of the organization confirmed that is how he started early in his entrepreneurial career, acknowledging, "I didn't have any college education when I started my businesses. I'll be honest with you, I just said screw it and jumped in with both feet, and let's see what happens. A lot of that is hard truth and hard knocks. I had to configure some sort of mentality of how I was going to survive. Really it becomes a trick because if you don't have it at the right place at the right time, chances are you're not, so lucky."

He has since sold his business after reaching hundreds of employees and major companies as clients. He then went to

---

38   Riley Panko, "Why Small Businesses Lack Accounting Resources in 2018," Clutch Report (blog), Clutch, October 1, 2018.

further his education to become a professor and now runs a successful business hub that educates business owners and prepares them through every stage of their business through an incubator program. Michael started Bam Biz Hub primarily to support the business owners that are unprepared, as he recognizes he was when he started his first business. He confesses that "I didn't know everything when I started my manufacturing business. In fact, I knew very little. But I hired all the right people around me and made sure I was very successful. You have to learn who those people are." Michael and his business partner Angel are working toward giving small business owners in the Permian Basin one place to go when they need assistance.

Examining the financial education needed to start a business and the emotional support needed to maintain the business, and the financial tools needed to make disciplined financial decisions is necessary for entrepreneurship.

Thirty-three percent of entrepreneurs have a high school diploma, and out of the rest, only 9 percent have their bachelor's degree. According to TSheets, reported by small biz geniuses, out of the 9 percent, three-fourths of them have a few business classes with no business education.[39]

The University of South Florida published an article reporting that the US Department of Treasury defines financial education proficiency as earning, spending, saving, borrowing, and protecting. The researchers of this study wanted to

---

39 "39 Entrepreneur Statistics You Need to Know in 2021," Smallbizgenius, accessed March 1, 2021.

emphasize the importance of financial education as it relates to the accounting field of business owner's education in the form of their ability to read financial statements and how it connects with the guidelines set by the US Department of Treasury. Identifying "This skill, while important to investors, is critical to people who have a small business."[40]

The business owner's financial understanding plays a large role in the flexibility of assets and, more importantly, cash, which is significant in accessing capital, investing back into the business, and financial planning. The business owner's understanding of basic financial concepts can assist in financial decisions and their access to capital. Banks and investors use this in their lending decisions. Peer-reviewed literature suggests individuals with more financial knowledge are more likely to engage in a wide range of recommended financial practices.[41] The general pattern of inadequacies documented in this journal with respect to debt and money management among consumers is apparently paralleled by comparable deficiencies for entrepreneurs.[42] This association between inadequate financial literacy and avoidance of financial statements was a recurring theme through the interviews of this case study. It attests to the connection between financial literacy and overall business success.[43]

---

40   Russell Sarder, "What is the main reason standard accounting principles are not useful?" December 11, 2018, video,:35 https://www.youtube.com/watch?v=I8NG-y9hdEU, accessed January 23, 2021.

41   Pearl Dahmen and Eileen Rodríguez, "Financial Literacy and the Success of Small Businesses: An Observation from a Small Business Development Center," Numeracy 7, Iss. 1 (2014): Article 3.

42   Ibid

43   Ibid

Knowledge is relevant in overcoming difficulties in accessing and managing credit markets. For example, financial literacy can facilitate the decision-making processes, such as payment of bills on time, proper debt management, which can improve the creditworthiness of potential borrowers to support firm performance. Therefore, the importance of being financial literate cannot be overemphasized with so many responsibilities we have in managing our business.

How do you manage your daily activities, including financial management?

Most small business owners have not been introduced to the usefulness of financial statements and financial ratios, and I can recognize this when I start working with a new customer. They don't know what they don't know, but unfortunately, this is not an excuse. It is important as business owners to get past our weaknesses and find solutions to overcome them.

It is the lack of educational desire that has categorized curiosity as an insensibility. Our spark has dwindled over time and has replaced our challenges and educational behaviors with fear and self-made obstacles. *The Science & Education Journal* published the article "Promoting Curiosity?" where the author Markus Lindholm suggests when we are young, curiosity and wonder are triggered by perceptive beauty rather than by facts. As a toddler, our curiosity is encouraged by exploring the diversity of the world. As a teenager, curiosity is ignited by a balance of lived experiences and educational models.[44]

As adults, we lose curiosity and our desire to learn for the pursuit of an elegant, individualistic lifestyle. What we start to lose is our imagination and wonder. Markus Lindholm promotes that wonder reflects the experience of naked existence beyond words and rather addresses the framework of our knowledge.[45] For example, one does not wonder what time it is but what time is, or for a business owner, don't just worry about profit but find the best way to secure financial leverage by validating your competitive advantage.

When our curiosity is filled by the fact that we think we know enough, or wonder must nourish our interest to learn. I came across an amazing statistic that at five years old, 98 percent of all children have no problem thinking individually. Most three-year-olds, on average, ask their parents about one hundred questions a day.[46]

Whoa! Every day!

44 Markus Lindholm, "Promoting curiosity?" Science & Education 27, no. 9–10 (2018): 987–1002.

45 R. Dawkins, Unweaving the rainbow: science, delusion and the appetite for wonder, New York: Teachers College Press, (1998). Opdal, P. M., Curiosity, wonder and education seen as perspective development, Studies in Philosophy and Education, 20, 331–344, (2001). Egan, K., Cant, A., & Judson, G., Wonder-full education: the centrality of wonder in teaching and learning across the curriculum, New York: Routledge, (2014).

46 Robert Stokoe, "Curiosity, a condition for learning," The International Schools Journal 32, no. 1 (2012): 63.

However, by the age of eleven, we pretty much stop asking, and by twenty-five, only 2 percent of people can think creatively. Curiosity seldom survives into adulthood.[47] So it's no wonder, no pun intended, that the more curious the business owner, the greater the chance of innovation, creativity, and financial understanding. Curiosity is the most superficial of all affections. It has an appetite that is very sharp but very easily satisfied.[48]

---

47 Ibid
48 E. Burke, "A philosophical enquiry into the origin of our ideas of the sublime and beautiful," London. Routledge & Kegan Paul. (1958. Original work published 1757).

CHAPTER 3

FUTURE BELONGS TO THE CURIOUS

––––

The intangible superpower of curiosity is available to everyone, yet not everyone uses it to their advantage. We are shaped by our experiences with our parents, our environment, and other people's perceptions of us, and we reduce acting on our curiosity to protect ourselves from the chances of failure and to not lose acceptance from others. Consequently, this decreases our chances for success because when we do not exercise our curiosity, we lose the opportunity to gain knowledge and develop our cognitive behaviors. Avoiding our curiosity can reduce our decision-making abilities and can lead to hardships. Information is vital to the confidence it takes to run a business because sometimes it can feel like a financial house of cards. One pull of a card and BAM! Everything crashes down. Just like in business, everything must balance.

When we ask other professionals for advice, enforce an hour of quiet time with no noise, read, write, or anything with an intentional focus on the information we put into our minds adds to our ability to make decisions, especially the financial decisions necessary to run a business.

Studies show curiosity can give us the emotional efficacy and financial literacy necessary to run a stable business. If curiosity is mandatory in running a financially judicious business, then *why is curiosity not emphasized more in education and in our workplace to heighten our development as people?* George Lowenstein's theory in the article "The wick in the candle of learning" explains the guide of their research is that curiosity arises from an incongruity or 'information gap'—a discrepancy between what one knows and what one wants to know.[49]

The theory assumes curiosity happens when someone wants to know something new. The level of knowledge increases sharply with small increases in knowledge. The information gap never really closes. It's just when we feel sufficiently knowledgeable and we feel sanctified, our curiosity evaporates. Curiosity is like hunger to our stomach. It reminds us of when we're hungry. Our thoughts and actions to our brain lead us to a hunger for knowledge, and small, "priming doses" of new knowledge increases the hunger and develop a habit of feeding yourself new information consistently.[50]

---

49 George Loewenstein, "The psychology of curiosity: a review and reinterpretation," *Psychological Bulletin*, 116 (1994), 75–98.

50 MJ Kang, et al., The Wick in the Candle of Learning: Epistemic Curiosity Activates Reward Circuitry and Enhances Memory, Psychological Science, 2009;20(8):963–973. doi:10.1111/j.1467–9280.2009.02402.x.

The decrease in curiosity is like being satiated by information. So, we feed on enough information our stomachs are full, accordingly.[51]

Curiosity is something that needs to be encouraged with an intentional focus. We will discover the benefits of feeding our curiosity outweigh the commitment needed to support our emotional and financial well-being. There are so many advantages you gain from curiosity, such as it increases our creativity, we become more empathetic, and we have more self-control. I could go on for pages listing all the benefits improving our curiosity can provide us. However, we will focus on the advantages that are more vital to our business success.

Imagine holding your baby, and they are grabbing your nose with one hand full of carrots and trying to pry your mouth open with the other to look inside as if your mouth opened into the milky way. Or when you take a glimpse into the rearview mirror, and you see your kid in the car seat amazed by all the new scenery, as if everything is being painted stroke by stroke as you drive down the road. Now imagine having that same insatiable desire toward everything you do as a business owner. That desire from within to want to know and see and ask about everything around us as babies and children is what we need to spark back up as young adults and adults.

The focal point is to explain how curiosity can upgrade our inner stability as entrepreneurs and business owners.

---

51   Ibid.

Running a business can be complicated. We put in late nights and early mornings, and every dime we have is seemingly handed over and invested into our dream. That is why I believe curiosity can have such an incredible impact on our business by motivating us to search for inner sensibility, confidence and encourages us to engage with others. Igniting your curious mind as a business owner and entrepreneur can be greatly beneficial in these areas:

- Curiosity can enhance your memory; it increases activity in our brain.
- Curiosity promotes innovativeness, necessary in a globally competitive market.
- Curiosity encourages a positive mindset, and positive mental health leads to positive results.
- Curiosity improves our relationships, a healthy approach to connecting with people.

These characteristics are not only important to our personal improvement, but they prove to be vital to our development into a successful business owner. Everyone can restore the desire to learn, and the fact is we can accomplish this for free by changing or tweaking some of our personal habits. The approach we will concentrate on comes at relatively no cost and produces a tremendous return individually and on how we implement our executive functions. All it takes is the willpower to concentrate on our unique skills.

A study by UCLA stated that five-year-old children ask sixty-five questions a day, whereas a forty-four-year-old adult asks six questions a day.[52]

Seriously, what are we really learning if we only ask ourselves a handful of questions a day?

We acquire our skills of curiosity at an early age, and it is molded by our experiences with our parents, the environment we live in, and our education. We are taught at an early age by our parents, and as we grow, it transitions into our friends in our neighborhood, and then when we enter the educational system, we are influenced by friends outside our neighborhood and teachers. Studies show if the parent doesn't stay engaged with the child, they will lose their appreciation for education. Research also shows curiosity declines if the parents don't stay involved in the child's education.

As society grew larger, the number of students per instructor, along with the traditional model of respect for authority, together put restrictions on the original child-to-parent question and answer educational relationship. This model resulted in an essentially one-way transfer of knowledge pattern from the instructor to the student with the resulting effect of diminishing the student's natural curiosity.

---

52   Jim Canterucci, Personal brilliance: Mastering the everyday habits that create a lifetime of success, New York: AMACOM Books, (2005).

The emphasis was on memorization from "chalk and talk" lectures.[53]

The encouragement for curiosity is based on the benefits that create positive thinking, guiding emotional persistence and optimistic actions, ultimately influencing our financial position. As business owners, we need to develop a grounded confidence, and it takes time, patience, and self-control. There are many ways to improve ourselves, whether we have the resources or not. Curiosity can enhance our lives through digging deep inside our gut and adding one or two new activities to our daily routine, such as:

- Find a quiet place and read a book, magazine, or listen to an audiobook. Reading can reduce stress, increase our mental endurance, and strengthen our decision-making. Statistics report 72 percent of Americans read at least one book in the last year, and the average daily reading time is around twelve minutes. The average person spends twenty-five dollars a year on books. A public library offers access to books, magazines, movies, and most libraries have access to audiobooks and books online with a library account.
- Find a quiet place to sit and be silent. It can be as simple as that, sit in silence and listen to your breath. Turn the brain off for a bit. Completely shut down for a while. I once heard there was a monk who could sit in silence for hours and not even have one thought. It's hard, but answers find us in silence. Unplug from technology.

---

53   Bussakorn Binson, "Curiosity-Based Learning (CBL) Program," Online *Submission* 6, no. 12 (2009): 13–22.

- Study a new topic. This led to me writing this book. I started reflecting on my past influences in my life, and I found curiosity was a common theme throughout my life. It sent me down a rabbit hole of studying curiosity, business concepts, and creating a solution for small business owners. This can be a powerful path to take.
- Find like-minded people to join forces with. Building partnerships is essential in business. It is a good idea to keep company with people who reinforce our goals and add positive actions to our lives. Build relationships by joining volunteer organizations that help in your community, which can be a great place to meet people who share the same passions as you.
- Ask more questions. This is a very powerful way to learn new information. I find it helpful when I'm on phone calls with business owners to ask them about the economics around their location. This helps me better understand what things are like in their area to understand the risk when helping fund the business or future businesses in the same area.

We make excuses in our lives by saying we don't have time for these things, but practicing these patterns can help assist in the development of our executive functions. This handful of suggestive habits of curiosity will develop more positive decision-making over time. It will, more importantly, help you create a more "grounded confidence" to know the difference.

Curiosity is also linked to positively enhancing our innovativeness. Entrepreneurial curiosity is defined as a positive emotional/motivational system oriented toward investigation in the entrepreneurial framework to learn tasks related to entrepreneurship and incorporate new experiences to improve business.[54] In 2016, a group of Slovenian professors performed a study on 331 entrepreneurs from the USA (52.3 percent) and Slovenia (47.7 percent). The purpose of this study was to see if curiosity and innovation shared a relationship in motivating the entrepreneur to learn about their business and how inclined they were to incorporate it into their entrepreneurial process. Innovation is an important driver in the evolution of the business and can help identify pain points in the business that need to be upgraded and can ease the crisis points during the ever-changing development of the business.

In this research, the values and systems of innovative companies versus those that were not mattered in that those that are not innovative do not search for new solutions and are not inward-looking in actively trying to improve their work, product, and services.

In the *Long-Range Planning Journal*, two researchers wrote a paper titled "Five Stages of Growth in Small Business" in which they state, "the transition from one stage to the next requires change, it will be accompanied by some crisis or another. Crises tend to be disruptive, and the problems of

54 Mitja Jeraj, "Toward the new construct; Entrepreneurial Curiosity," V D. Barkovic and B. Runzheimer (ur.), *Interdisciplinary research VIII* (p. 1043–1055), Opatija: Josip Juraj Strossmayer University in Osijek. (2012).; Mitja Jeraj & B. Antončič, "A Conceptualization of Entrepreneurial Curiosity and Construct Development: A Multi-Country Empirical Validation," Creativity *Research Journal*, 25(4), 426–435, http://dx.doi.org/10.1 080/10400419.2013.843350. (2013).; Mitja Jeraj & Miha Maric, "Entrepreneurial Curiosity—The New Construct. *High potentials, lean organization, internet of things: proceedings of the 32nd International Conference on Organizational Science Development*," (str. 289–298). Kranj: Moderna organizacija. (2013b).

change can be minimized if managers are proactive rather than reactive. Prior knowledge of what generates crises and what to expect in each stage will smooth the process of change."[55] Innovation is a required attribute the entrepreneur needs to reduce the uncertainties during change and increase opportunities to enhance the business.

During the Slovenian study, the entrepreneurs were asked to fill out a series of questions that measure their innovativeness using the Jackson Personality Inventory Manual, "which defines innovativeness as a tendency to be creative in thought and action, and was used to capture this construct as innovation, creativity, and initiative have been consistently identified as one of the enduring characteristics of entrepreneurs."[56]

A couple of examples of these statements were:

FOR INNOVATIVENESS:
I obtain more satisfaction from mastering a skill than coming up with a new idea.

---

55 Mel Scott and Richard Bruce, "Five Stages of Growth in Small Business," Long Range Planning 20, no. 3, 45–52.

56 Stephen L. Mueller and Anisya S. Thomas, "Culture and entrepreneurial potential: A nine country study of locus of control and innovativeness," *Journal of business venturing* 16, no. 1 (2001): 51–75. Stephen L. Mueller and Anisya S. Thomas, "Culture and entrepreneurial potential: A nine country study of locus of control and innovativeness," *Journal of business venturing* 16, no. 1 (2001): 51–75.

FOR ENTREPRENEURIAL CURIOSITY:
When I notice an abandoned building, I think about what business potential it represents for me.

The subjects were to label their relation to the statement from one to seven. A rating of one for strongly disagree and up to seven for strongly agree. The results were similar between the two countries, and it demonstrated "that in the frame of entrepreneurship psychology entrepreneurial curiosity is important for innovativeness."[57] As the global market continues to threaten the preservation of small businesses, innovation is an influential aspect in defending our position in the economy. "Since entrepreneurs with higher levels of entrepreneurial curiosity gather more data and knowledge, they should transform this base of applicable knowledge with innovativeness" to better the results of their companies.[58]

The study found higher levels of entrepreneurial curiosity led to higher levels of innovativeness. In this study, it was identified those who were entrepreneurially curious understood change and, more importantly, how to navigate through change. We can all recognize the impact technological innovation has had on our society, and we can only expect that to increase. Curiosity can help create more innovative processes through the knowledge we attain over time, business partnerships through the relationships we create, and as we get exposed to more information, we are more creative in finding solutions instead of problems.

---

57 Ziga Peljko, Mitja Jeraj, Gheorghe Săvoiu, and Miha Marič, "An empirical study of the relationship between entrepreneurial curiosity and innovativeness," *Organizacija* 49, no. 3 (2016).

58 Ibid.

What we learn more through this research is "the ability to be innovative represents to entrepreneurs and their companies a relative advantage in relation to entrepreneurs that lack innovativeness."[59] So I would promote taking time to read, in general, or just trying to learn more each day. Time for the brain to work naturally through silence like reading and meditation is closely linked to the next advantage of curiosity.

Another advantage curiosity can give us is a positive mindset.

Society has created a business mindset that if we're not making money, then we're wasting time. It is at the expense of our peace of mind, but financial peace starts with emotional peace. My father told me he thought my ideas were great, but when would he have found time to do that. He said he was busy trying to make money to pay the bills. I would've rather had him around the house more.

Growing up, I admired my father's ambition. He had a fearless motivation to be his own boss. As a business owner, he was a fantastic salesman. He was very engaged with everyone he saw. Every day he wore a pressed shirt, and I can still remember the sound of his legs searching for the bottom of the pant leg through his heavily starched dockers.

He made sure to look as profitable as he hoped to be someday. In spite of his determination, the energy that he left with every morning didn't quite make it home with him, and some days neither did he. He had an inner drive to chase the

---

59   Ibid.

American dream of a reliable, continuous income to support the family and devote more time at home.

I believe the answer fell in the lines of psychologist Glen Moriarty's quote when he said, "The bigger the gap between where you are and your expectations of where you should be, the higher the stress."[60] The Mindset Project was created by Michael DeVenney, a man who dealt with anxiety and depression during a large part of his entrepreneurial journey.

For business owners, this means keeping emotions out of our decision-making. The Mindset Project did a study that showed the number one cause that affected the reaction to our decision-making was when we dwell on our anxieties and fears during stress points in the business, stating "a loss of independent identity—Entrepreneurs equate their personal value and worth with the results of their business, far beyond the typical levels of role identity seen in other professions."[61]

A curious mindset also fosters an openness to others. When we become open to the advice of others, we create the ability to include everyone in the decision-making process, reducing flaws in the organization. When we focus on others, we take in ideas and recommendations that can assist us in making better decisions. If a business owner is primarily focused on individualistic desires, then they cannot see the values of others.

---

60 The Mindset Project, "At the Intersection of Entrepreneurship and Positive Mindset Part VI: Entrepreneurial Wellbeing as a Path to Business Success," Accessed August 31, 2020.

61 Ibid

Creative problem-solving occurs when employees challenge and cross-pollinate existing knowledge and approaches with new ideas.[62] Research demonstrates that framing work around learning goals (e.g., skill development) rather than performance goals (e.g., hitting targets) boosts motivation. Those motivated by learning goals tend to acquire a greater diversity of skills, do better in problem-solving, and log better work performance, although organizations generally prioritize performance goals, according to Harvard behavioral scientist Francesca Gino.[63] Leaders can counteract this trend by advocating for the importance of learning and by rewarding people both for their performance and the learning needed to get there.

Purpose and improved performance are created through internal processes and an understanding of the value the organization can bring. Maintaining a continuous review of operational processes, educating staff, and properly educating ourselves on the accounting systems can reduce the risk of financial problems because you are collecting financial data points that provide more information to make business decisions.

Preparation and proper financial tools are more reliable than our emotions when it comes to financial decision-making. When we build our positive curiosity, we begin to become more aware of the processes and patterns of our business, we are more engaged with our employees, we make decisions with a clear mind, and we are better at decision-making.

---

62   Francesca Gino, "The business case for curiosity," Harvard *Business Review* 96, no. 5 (2018): 48–57.

63   Ibid

These areas built over time can direct our patterns toward positive development. In the HBO documentary *Becoming Warren Buffett*, he says, "If you have an economic castle, people are going to want to take that castle away, and you better have a strong moat, and you better have a knight who knows what he's doing."[64] The moat is the intangibles of the business that protect the business, such as the internal processes, culture, brand, leadership, teamwork, economic alignment, and there must be a leader that recognizes that and knows how to protect the palace.

---

64 "Becoming Warren Buffett." directed by Peter W. Kunhardt. written by Chris Chuang. release date January 30, 2017.

CHAPTER 4

CONFIDENCE AND CURIOSITY

Curiosity is not only given to the rich and successful. It is given to everyone, but the problem is as humans, we let our emotions govern our decision-making. When we don't research and determine the true outcome, we let our minds wander into the negative things that can happen.

Curiosity is superficial in the sense it can arise, change focus, or end abruptly.[65]

I have seen the thinking process through the eye of the small business owner in many different aspects. Most small business owners are obsessed with money and taxes. That's all they ever talk about, never mind the inefficiencies, technology, and the culture of the business are not being addressed, ultimately losing cash and opportunities. I've seen business

---

65   George Loewenstein, "The psychology of curiosity: a review and reinterpretation," *Psychological Bulletin*, 116 (1994), 75–98.

owners spend business money just to reduce their tax liability and in the same year complain the business isn't thriving. It's a false sense of entitlement. They know as long as they can hold up with appearances, they'll be fine, but they are not spending an equal amount of time spent on the right things to create sustainable financial success. Such as:

1. Question business processes, both operational and "back office," and create a culture that is open to new ideas and challenge others to adopt new ways of working.
2. Understand each role in the organization and how they interact with each other.
3. Build internal and external partnerships and build strategic networks and alliances.
4. Recognize internal and external stakeholders and build relationships to both communicate opportunities and stabilize competing challenges.
5. Respect diversity, understand differences, and work toward a unified approach toward obstacles.
6. Perform positive strategic actions toward business.[66]

I've had the privilege of working with some incredible business owners in many different ways, both those that lead to success and to failure.

To help other business owners, I will discuss some of the most important things I've seen that helped people fight for their purpose. I wanted to demonstrate some of their best practices and what I've discovered from an impressive group of

---

66   Ellen Van Velsor, Patricia Hind, Andrew Wilson, and Gilbert Lenssen, "Developing leaders for sustainable business," *Corporate Governance: The international journal of business in society* (2009).

owners with an intense interest to grow fueled by their desire to learn. Curiosity has always been linked to exploration for a hidden passion, query, or inspiration insights. Today, it is even more linked to a life-journey style and future foresight. With curiosity, the socioeconomic issues can see practices that do creation, communication, and commercialization of meaningful, unique ideas.[67]

During my study into small businesses, I've discovered obstacles small business owners face are universal, but everyone feels alone when going through them. Over time, the small business survival rate decreases. Failure is often harder on entrepreneurs who lose money they've borrowed on credit cards or from friends and relatives than it is on those who raised venture capital.

"When you've bootstrapped a business where you're not drawing a salary and depleting whatever savings you have, that's one of the very difficult things to do," says Toby Stuart, a professor at the Haas School of Business at the University of California, Berkeley.[68]

The most common reasons are issues created internally throughout the life of the business that never gets addressed properly. Such as:

- Businesses that start undercapitalized have a greater chance of failure than firms that start with adequate capital.

---

67   Mohamed Buheji, "Designing a Curious Life," AuthorHouse, UK. (2019).
68   Deborah Gage, "The venture capital secret: 3 out of 4 start-ups fail," Wall Street Journal 20 (2012).

- Businesses that do not keep updated and accurate records and do not use adequate financial controls have a greater chance of failure than firms that do.
- Businesses that do not develop specific business plans have a greater chance of failure than firms that do.
- Businesses that do not use professional advisors have a greater chance of failure than firms using professional advisors.

With small businesses making up a majority of all US businesses, it is important to address the leading cause of small business closures, which is a lack of financial education. The most common message being advertised is a "work harder than your competition" mindset, but without a right mix of passion and a strong desire to learn, small business closures will remain high.

I never knew why emotions would get in the way of success, but that is the largest lesson to learn. We need to find emotional awareness and control the marathon of thoughts constantly running through our heads. It wasn't until I accepted my curiosity as a blessing that it turned everything around for me emotionally.

Curiosity is shown to create a perceptive nature because of the openness to receiving information. When we are open to learning, we are more likely to find solutions to some of the most complex obstacles we personally struggle with. As curiosity researchers show, the result is an expanded problem-solving tool kit so we can better handle the distress or negative emotions associated with the challenges of our driven pursuits.

When we allow this contradicting voice in our minds to override our truth, we get lost in other people's reality because our actions are not led by our principles. When we as business owners don't follow our principles, we are convinced money and profits are the only determinants to success. Therefore, business owners who don't get a grasp of their emotions will fall victim to the psychological rollercoaster according to their bottom line.

Currently, emotional intelligence (EI) is defined as a type of social intelligence that involves "the ability to monitor one's own and others' emotions, to discriminate among them, and to use the information to guide one's thinking and actions."[69] With regard to these processes, it is suggested individuals develop skills and abilities pertaining to the perception of emotions, the regulation of emotions, and the capacity to utilize or reason with emotions in thought.[70]

This orientation yields a form of resiliency that enables people to be more innovative and creative to solve problems.

In a recent study by Mohamed Buheji for the *American Journal of Economics*, he measured curiosity by the level of imaginal processes inventory (IPI) you get from questioning, investigating, trying, testing, and learning the processes as an attempt to solving the world's problems.[71] Mohamed

69 Peter Salovey and John D. Mayer, "Emotional intelligence," Imagination, *cognition and personality* 9, no. 3 (1990): 185–211.

70 John D. Mayer, Peter Salovey, D. R. Caruso, and R. J. Sternberg, "Models of emotional intelligence," *Emotional intelligence: Key readings on the Mayer and Salovey model* (2000): 81–119.

71 Mohamed Buheji, "Optimising the 'Economics of Curiosity' for Better Future Foresight," (2020): 21–28.

Buheji states without equity, diversity, and inclusion, we can never fully reach such a level of curiosity as seen with the creations of the futuristic business models we see today.

If Elon Musk did not include others, providing a wide variety of opinions, he would not be able to create some of the wildest inventions we see today. We can clearly link financial success with people's level of curiosity through the technological creation we see in today's capital-driven economy. Still, the questions being asked from a curiosity perspective are "Does this provide real growth?" and "Do these creations address human needs to thrive?"

In 2004, *The Journal of Personality Assessment* noted curiosity was conceptualized as a positive emotional-motivational system associated with the recognition, pursuit, and self-regulation of novelty and challenge.[72]

How do curious driven business owners lead the future?

They free themselves from the blind spots created in their mind from a fixed mindset by not having preconceived solutions, and they use their curiosity to hurdle over gratification traps that develop through complacency. They use their imagination to find creative future solutions using new

---

72 Todd B. Kashdan, Paul Rose, and Frank D. Fincham, "Curiosity and exploration: Facilitating positive subjective experiences and personal growth opportunities," Journal *of personality assessment* 82, no. 3 (2004): 291–305.

approaches, data, and curiosity to reflect future outcomes and results.

Alison Horstmeyer explains that people find their work more meaningful when they create positive results that are fulfilling to their own values, competence, positive self-regard, and have a connection to the organization. She goes on to say, "one-way business leaders can help themselves and employees enhance the meaningfulness of their work is by adopting a curious mindset." The development of learning can help decrease the failure rate as the business ages through a desire for improvement. A curious mindset will help you find your conviction but, more importantly, will also help you create the foundation for how you'll position yourself to magnify your conviction.

One reason curiosity is carried out by the most successful business owners is because it encourages perseverance over obstacles, achieving goals, and challenging themselves to develop enhanced skills. The mindset helps develop effort and focus on one's abilities to create solutions over obstacles that at times seem impossible to overcome.

The curious mindset helps expand our imagination and awareness for the future. You can really see this during the start-up of the business. Every entrepreneur starts off with a determination and persistence that is fascinating, even when there is no evidence of their success. If we maintain a high level of curiosity throughout the life of the business, we get a higher sense of purpose for our business and the people we work with.

Human motivation has been linked to curiosity as a source of development and emotional intelligence. Incorporating an inviting environment of cooperation and communication toward expected financial responsibilities produces an investment into human motivation that will help during financial hardships. However, losing interest over time can create a complacent mindset and lead to financial distress because it leads to a reactive approach to problem-solving. A curious mindset can increase the chance of creativity to develop solutions and find reliable opportunities for growth.

As a business progresses through the different stages of growth, it is a useful practice to document your thinking. This will help develop the little nuggets of information as you continue creating the decision-making process. When we focus on the progression of the business without documenting the strategy, it causes us to rely too much on our memory. With documentation, we can visually see our progress now that we have a proactive approach to achieving success. When we document our approach through the business growth, we develop a common focus for ourselves and our team. It is not enough to expect others to interpret our demands. We must create an environment that embraces constant communication.

Scientists have discovered various ways to enhance a desire to learn based on challenging yourself to expand beyond your sensitivity level, which includes embracing communication. The 2019 *Journal of Nursing Education* highlighted how curiosity and interpersonal communication could be viewed as asking more empathetic questions + curiosity + practice = grounded confidence, which comes down to meaning if you practice the skills of having challenging conversations along with exercising a curiosity to learn, then you will build a "grounded confidence" necessary to be an effective leader in the workplace.[73]

Curiosity can build our creativity, communication with others, and gives us confidence by using our imagination, but the study is just now being researched. Could it be we confuse using our imagination as childish? Curiosity is a behavioral trait most of us are lucky to experience as a child and can be seen up until the age of seven. It is said to dissolve once we become molded by our environment, parents, and the educational system. We stop believing in our imagination and creativity and start questioning everything through fear.

We choose to stay inside of ourselves and stop exploring the world because we'd rather be right than ask questions and look like we don't know something, especially when it comes to business. If we do not have challenging conversations with others, then how will we learn and create new solutions?

Research finds entrepreneurs lack the financial literacy important to business success. There are many different reasons people do not create that understanding. It highlights poor financial acumen and management errors. It shows the undeveloped potential that was so high at the beginning of the business. A willing emotional passion is not enough. It's just as necessary for owners to maintain an interest in evaluating the financial position of the business regularly.

---

73   Brené Brown, Dare to Lead: Brave Work. Tough Conversations, Whole Hearts, Random House, 2018.

In business and in life, when we exercise our curiosity, we can improve our decision-making and creativity in creating financial processes that help us succeed. Decision-making in children is original and authentic. They use two categorical approaches toward making decisions: exploration choices and exploitation choices. An exploration choice is usually a slower decision where we gather enough information and improve our knowledge to make a sound decision. An exploitative choice is where we choose the best option based on the information we have at the time.

The problem with an exploitative choice is it usually means we didn't gather enough data, and we're trying to make a decision "on the fly." What a curious mindset does is it gets us interested enough to gather data little by little over time, which leads us to have a grounded confidence in every choice we make. Warren Buffett once said in an interview he creates a simple decision-making process where he collects as much information as he can about each deal and only compares it to any other available deal available at the time.

He practices the information gap theory—a discrepancy between what one knows and what one wants to know in that small doses of information over time greatly increase curiosity. When we are reading, writing, and asking questions, we increase our chances of making the right choices when we make business decisions.[74]

---

74 George Loewenstein, "The psychology of curiosity: a review and reinterpretation," Psychological *Bulletin, 116* (1), 75–98. (1994).

Curiosity leads to better cognition and leads to a higher, more intellectual business decision-maker. Even though there is not a lot of understanding of the inner meaning of curiosity, research shows there are two driving forces for adult exploration and curiosity where we get our motivation to gather information and is the internal "desire" toward cognitive development.

The goal of developing curiosity is stimulating your brain with the reward kicks it needs to develop the proper processes and structure in the business. Not only are we using data to calculate our taxes or when we need a loan to fund a project, but also using our own business data to constantly make adjustments to the business to maximize success.

The intangible aspects of our business should be one of the most focused portions of the business because those are the areas, we gather information, and this is where we can build value as long as we build learning capacity to make use of it. The benefits of accumulating information may not have an immediate impact, but the delayed benefits require a process of learning.

In the collection of information, we can close the gap in knowledge and understanding because we can use small doses of information that will continue to increase curiosity. Science shows we are more curious when we have some idea of how something works. As we gather more information over time, our confidence to make choices strengthens. After a time, that information turns into better choices, more efficient search, and more sophisticated comparisons, and it brings an advanced visualization of success.

Curiosity builds better models and information tradeoffs, and business is an information tradeoff. Curiosity opens the value of options because it opens your thought process to see every opportunity as an option. Curiosity can minimize risk because of the information gathered. The gathering of information leads us to a better understanding of what opportunities we choose to work toward.

I followed a study that looked at what is happening to our decision-making in the real world when we are faced with decisions. What they uncovered was the reward mechanism provided when we are faced with challenges does not get stimulated very often because big life making decisions don't happen every day. They found curiosity can help trigger this reward mechanism by exploring our environment and developing new skills.

I use my mouse to my computer with the opposite dominant hand some days just to trigger a tad more focus into my day. The study from the Graduate University for Advanced Studies and the National Institute of Informatics in Tokyo, Japan, shows an alternative approach to motivating us to explore innovative patterns using curiosity and the ability to acquire new skills which might become useful for the future.

Curiosity is motivated by the early human stage of development: babies reward themselves for acquiring increasingly difficult new skills.[75]

---

75 Nicolas Bougie and Ryutaro Ichise, "Skill-based curiosity for intrinsically motivated reinforcement learning," Machine *Learning* 109, no. 3 (2020): 493–512.

Business owners are faced with difficult decisions that affect the business in one way or another toward success and profitability or decline and distress. As a business owner, it is important to set goals as we'll discuss how goal-conditioned learning policies optimize rewards and incentives toward new goals and new information. In turn, it produces new skills, which the research from Japan shows that new skills are mastered when we can achieve our goals in confidence. As we gain momentum from achieving our goals, our confidence builds, and the cycle of success starts.

The researchers introduce us to a new model derived from curiosity called the goal-based curiosity module (GCM) that states we interact within our environment by performing actions, and these actions lead to an external reward. As we learn how to receive this external reward, we then create policies or a set of actions that enhances the occurrence of these rewards through curiosity and the exploration of complicated states.[76]

These human behaviors toward goals are the same in our financial behavior toward our financial goals. If we do not collect the financial data within the business and we are not monitoring profitability to identify financial holes and pinpoint opportunities, then what chance are we giving ourselves to succeed?

As a result, curiosity incentivizes the agent to seek new knowledge and discover new skills that might lead to the

---

76   Ibid.

final goal.[77] These new skills are knowledge of new financial metrics, understanding the financial health of the business, and actively protecting the business's competitive advantage. As we use our curiosity to develop new skills, we are able to not only achieve distant goals but we can also accomplish multiple goals.[78]

One way curiosity does this is that when we are faced with financial decisions for the business, we are better prepared because we build a consistent buildup of new information that leads to new skills. Therefore, implementing consistent financial evaluation of the business is important to reach the goals of the business owner. The use of financial statements is critical because this provides the barometer to whether or not the business is profitable and sustainable.

Warren Buffett's curiosity toward financial statements is what he has acknowledged as one of his strengths as a businessman and one of the reasons why he became one of the richest men in the world. Why are small business owners not taught how to understand financial statements and financial metrics?

My assumption is there is a lot of money made off these businesses failing. The ability for banks to charge interest off of loans, the chance for investors to scoop up businesses cheaply because of mis-financial management and gather assets for pennies on the dollar when the business owner has already stretched his last penny.

---

77   Ibid.
78   Ibid.

The business owner's lack of financial literacy and the emotional connection to money creates a vulnerability to the business. There has been a rise in celebrity business coaches teaching the newest psychology to exploit the business owners' fears to charge outrageous amounts of money for vague advice from new age philosophies. Academic research shows business coaches actually have no impact on the bottom line. What they found is it is more of an emotional exchange, and if the business owner feels that it is working, then it is working.

If we can spend the time necessary to learn a little bit each day about our operations of our business over time, we will be more engaged and devoted more to the success of the business. My father fell victim to the "hustler" mindset and thought if he wasn't working, then he wasn't making money, but if he had only understood to build the business by monitoring it from a higher business point of view, it could've saved his business. My father took for granted that the finances were being managed by his business partner, but in the end, he was spinning his wheels in the accounts receivable hamster wheel.

He was continuously doing work for people who hadn't paid him in months, and when capital is low, and he tried to collect on invoices from months back, and it put a financial strain on the life of his business. His lack of curiosity in monitoring the financial health consistently became the downfall of his successful business because he did not become proactively aware of the financial stressors in his business.

CHAPTER 5

DARE TO BE CURIOUS

———

As a child, I couldn't understand the stress of running a business. However, in hindsight, I could tell you when my father's business wasn't doing well.

I saw a connection between financial stability and the self-control of my clients. Money is a stressor for business owners, and it is hard to make decisions effectively. There is an overwhelming feeling of running a business, and it only increases as you're losing money from mismanagement of systems, cash, and time.

The smaller the business, the harder it is to manage because money is so closely tied to personal financial comfort. My dad wasn't alone in turning to self-destructive habits and causing more disruption to the cohesion of the business.

How many times a day do you see business coaches flooding your social media, providing a glimpse into the glitz and glam of how they portray their *success*? You see them jumping on a jet, creating the illusion they are off to a fancy destination to close a deal or off to a vacation you could only dream of taking, but it's a joke. They create so much content that, of course, anyone could and would eventually learn something from them, but as the old saying goes, "the sun shines on a dog's ass occasionally."

Take this from Wisdomfuel.com, a group of ambitious learners who assess the most sought-after business programs. They research educational courses and weed out the scammers.[79] They state anyone can get value out of it, but not everyone will see that value as a fair trade for the amount they're paying. They go on to describe the quality of the teachings are inconsistent. These business coaches create the illusion of being a guru in sales and claim they can unlock the hidden treasures "buried in a cave," such as Indiana Jones finding the Ark of the Covenant. The message from these people is sales can fix anything, and, in turn, money fixes everything.

Ha!

We've already discussed that no matter what level of income you make, it is so important to have your emotions in check because money can and will create more problems. I once worked for a gentleman who was extremely successful, well-read, healthy, spiritual, and he still couldn't control his emotions. Every day was a different mood, and it caused confusion with the business strategy, distrust, and a lot of pointed fingers between employees.

79 "Cardone University Review—Is Grant Cardone Legit?" Wisdomfuel, accessed October 4, 2020.

We cannot expect courses to solve our true character flaws or provide the experience of learning the right lessons for ourselves. The characteristics can only be attained through curiosity, a lot of trial and error, and emotional stability through:

- **Social Curiosity.** Social curiosity is about being involved with social issues and being able to connect effectively during a social gathering or event. Social curiosity helps to discover opportunities ingrained within the community.
- **Emotional Curiosity.** Curiosity can be described as positive emotions toward acquiring knowledge. Discovering new information may also be rewarding because it can help reduce undesirable states of uncertainty.
- **Resilience Curiosity.** Resilience curiosity flourishes when we start the reasoning stage of what we experience. With active experimentation or experiential learning, we start the curiosity journey of socioeconomic problem-solving and a positive mindset.
- **Innovation Curiosity.** Innovation-driven curiosity can come from different dimensions. Excessive anxiety impedes human lust for new discovery. With innovation curiosity, we recognize and seek new information and experiences.
- **Problem Ambiguity Curiosity.** Curiously living with ambiguity means we will have an open mindset that manages the challenge of the new hypotheses while attempting to reduce the blind spots. Through ambiguity of any problem faced in life, we can build curiosity and thus avoid any negative thoughts.

The interest in using business coaches as an emphasis on business performance improvement is increasing in popularity.

However, there isn't any clear evidence that shows the benefit of using a business coach to achieve your goals. Studies have shown no universally accepted way of evaluating the added value because it is seen to be an emotional experience.

Owners are always looking for a performance edge, and this means they are looking for someone with the same experiences to share the same struggles and fears. There is nothing wrong with wanting to relate to someone and their experiences. However, many of the "get rich quick" coaches aren't guiding on proven business practices. There is little to no research provided on how to evaluate the direct impact of business coaching on someone's actual business, but the most impactful coaching indicated a beneficial influence of supervision during coaching.

During an interview I conducted for this book, as I discussed with Price Arredondo, director of small business for a state economic development department in Washington DC, he admitted much of the small business owners he is talking to are looking for someone to guide them through the business process from start-ups to existing companies.

Price describes his experience by saying, "A lot of the people who come to me generate a lot of revenue but are not good at managing money and understanding cash flow, understanding how to build relations with the banks if they need to expand, buy equipment, or just the necessity of having access to capital when they may need it. They're just not prepared to do that. They're not fully engaged in the business practices, they're not fully engaged with external organizations, or they are not investing in their innovation. To me, those are major deterrents to them building sustainability. It's difficult, but it's just that simple."

It is great to reach out to people like Price, and it is even more important we further educate ourselves to learn more about the professionals who are teaching us instead of just letting them do it for us. Once we get past the learning curve, we can better introduce them to our processes.

Especially to avoid getting caught up in the sophisticated "get rich" ads we see today, as Price Arredondo further explains, "Many times business owners tend to think the advice we provide doesn't work, but they forget these methods and advice we introduce them to must be put into action and constantly improved. They stop doing research. We walk them through a process where they can learn everything about their industry and where their industry is going. Is their business growing, and is their industry growing? What's that trend?"

A legitimate coaching relationship can have tremendous positive effects, but to date, there has been little attention paid to the possibility that coaching can also exhibit negative effects.[80] Carsten C. Schermuly and Carolin Graßmann studied the negative effects of business coaching. What they found was negative effects happened frequently, but only a few of them were severe, and most of them were low in intensity.

---

80 Carsten C. Schermuly and Carolin Graßmann, "A literature review on negative effects of coaching—what we know and what we need to know," Coaching: *An International Journal of Theory, Research and Practice* 12, no. 1 (2019): 39–66.

If the business owner thinks it's working, then it's working. This is mainly because the business owner is not always aware of what they are truly looking for.

Online business coaches continue to focus on the personal lifestyle, and business owners buy into an unsustainable lifestyle through an emotional feeling of success. Most of these coaches teach marketing and sales, causing people to fall prey to the lifestyle they see from the coaches' boorish social media posts. This causes problems not only for the relationship between mentor and mentee but for the overall outcome of the business and, in some cases, lead to personal discontent. People buy into these programs but blame themselves when they don't work.

The most common problem in this relationship is the expertise of the mentor, the protégé performance problems such as unwillingness to learn, interpersonal problems such as dependency, and destructive relational patterns such as jealousy.[81]

As a consultant, I experienced firsthand the negative effects of assisting clients in their businesses primarily due to the financial efficacy of the business owner. So, it was enlightening to see Schermuly provide research showing 59 percent of the clients who were coached either were not aware of their problem, had the wrong expectations of their problems, or had no goals to fix their problem.

81 L. T. Eby and McManus, S. E., "The protégés role in negative mentoring experiences," *Journal of Vocational Behavior, 65,* 255–275. (2004).

It is not totally the fault of the business owners. It is largely the fault of our education system because, in most cases, financial education is not taught in our schools. Specific social classes don't get a chance to receive a college education or have a family to help teach financial efficacy.

If the owner is not curious to learn more, the results are discouraging. From what I have seen, it was the clients who made the conscious effort and decision to learn and implement the necessary processes to improve their goals, understand financial statements, and focus on their personal well-being.

International Journal of Evidence Based Coaching and Mentoring published an article written by Mel Leedham in which he revealed there is a link between an individual's confidence and the business owner's performance, and coaching seems to improve confidence.[82] What these online business coaches understand is the psychological influence can create a feeling their advice is effective because if the business owner feels good, then they can substantiate the cost. Basically, any new positive changes that are implemented create a new sense of entrepreneurial intensity.

Only 7 percent of the 1100 business owners surveyed focused on the results and techniques from actual problems and established the skill development to fix the issues for the future.[83] The number one answer was confidence and

---

82 Melville Leedham, "The coaching scorecard: A holistic approach to evaluating the benefits of business coaching," PhD diss., Oxford Brookes University, 2004.

83 Ibid.

self-belief, so we are more inclined to trust ourselves, and the most successful owners focus on controlling their emotions and psychological growth.

It is more important to develop the necessary skills to learn financial effectiveness and build confidence. When we are more confident, we are more inclined to follow through with successful habits needed for maximum business performance.

There needs to be a tangible measurement to calculate whether the business coach is effective. It's not enough to get a "good" feeling when working with a business coach. A foundation needs to be formed through processes and accurate data collection to conclusively calculate results. Continuing the chapter, we will explore how you can calculate a return on investment.

The US business owner has been glamorized in the media as the perfect specimen of creation and success without focusing on the long-term effects of their financial decisions. News coverage, business articles, and social media feature lifestyle entrepreneurs who build an audience promoting life quality without promoting financial stability. New techniques focused on revenue and marketing are being created for the small business owner without any true guidance of implementing a stable business by properly using financial tools, implementing accounting policies to track data properly, and building curiosity toward the procedures of the business to maximize the effectiveness of the competitive advantage.

I saw a connection between the financial stability and the self-control of my clients. Money is a stressor for business owners, and it is hard to make decisions effectively. There is an overwhelming feeling of running a business, and it only increases as you're losing money from mismanagement of systems, cash, and time.

Business owners must compromise their time between the intangibles and tangibles both business and in life, bound by spending time at work, managing a family, team development, paying bills, and the list goes on. That's the point; our curiosity will encourage our thoughts and move us to action. Our curiosity to learn more information leads us to collect and sort this newly gained knowledge and sort it into rational bits of information we can piggy bank for future financial decision-making.

Through the unforgiving entrepreneurial mountain to the highest peak is personal well-being. The climb up to the peak is strenuous, but the ones who reach the top built a foundation on purpose and self-discipline. It's no different than climbing a real mountain. It requires preparation, execution, and support.

I think it should start with emotional support and financial literacy. Many of the conferences I attend on small business focus seem to be targeting the venture capital path to starting a business, such as how to create a business plan and how to create a pitch. Venture capital is a debt or equity strategy plan that most small business owners do not start with. There are still many small businesses that start with the money in their pocket and the sweat off their brow. For those business owners, it is important to advocate more for education.

In today's world, business owners need to understand the factors representing stage of growth, shareholder influence, product or service offering, customer demand, global reach, personnel expertise, and an ability to react swiftly to change the factors which impact the overall performance of the business.

With all the skills needed to run a business, time constraints, and a need for quick and ready frameworks, methodologies, and relevant answers to business imperatives, many entrepreneurs are neither willing to take time out to attend formal university training nor want to spend the energy accumulating knowledge not immediately useful.[84] However, lack of skill and knowledge can lead to entrepreneurial business owners facing pressures of isolation, limited feedback, or operational ineptitude.

Business coaches portray themselves as the professional in the field or the guru of the industry, but most of the time, they are merely highlighting recycled sales practices. What they have done is find psychological ways for business owners to buy into an unsustainable lifestyle. You get an emotional feeling of "we made it" when we can afford a lifestyle that others may never experience.

Small business owners without any true guidance of implementing a stable business highlight the spiritual, financial, and emotional strengths of being a business owner. Business owners are relying on this fake sense of power that they can get through anything because they created the business.

---

84 Ibid.

They are focusing on getting rich schemes to manage a fake lifestyle. What these business coaches understand is any change creates an emotional feeling of success, but studies have found there is no return on investment calculation on the cost of a business coach because it is an emotional feeling. If you feel the advice is working, then you'll always substantiate the cost.

However, you're not creating a stable business, just a lifestyle of things you don't need. They are focusing on the results and techniques that work on the masses, not individually. Once you receive their advice, you're paying thousands of dollars an hour on their word that can be used on any business. They are selling ideas that only they think they know; this lifestyle-focused mindset is working on your subconscious mind and convincing you that as long as you have everything you desire, you've made it.

The US business owner has been glamorized as the perfect specimen of creation, and we idolize their success without focusing on their long-term success. We don't pay attention to the long-term effects of these businesses because we're only focused on the now. The world is filled with a frantic amount of information, and as humans, we must not get lost in the jumbled and hurried pace that this knowledge is being targeted at us.

It's hard to focus on everything going on in our lives and when we add counterproductive noise and distractions. It is important to hone in on silence every day, on hectic days, and on slow days to reflect on the good and the bad to develop processes that are unique to our business. We can PREPARE for the future based on the information we learn from our stillness.

When attention is placed on the longevity and preparedness of the business, it can provide stability and recognition of our business's competitive advantage.

If we have a quick money mindset, it is a narrow mindset focusing on the tangibles of what the business provides, like money, rather than the intangibles it can capitalize on, like wealth. It is a mindset of "I" and not "we." Many of these online business programs are vague, so their message can appeal to a larger audience. It creates an economic shift for the content creators to create a lifestyle for themselves, hurting business owners in its path.

There has not been any research on the negative effects of a business coaches' advice because it is an emotional purchase. It is based on a high-energy emotion that creates a feeling of change and a mirage of success.

Every business has ups and downs, and it's how you position your processes within the company that aids in the fluctuation of owning a business. There isn't a focus in the company on the ideas of the employees. As a whole, it is more a top-tiered decision-making process where the owner makes the decision, and the employees perform the tasks.

However, if the owner doesn't understand the processes and dynamics of the workplace then the task cannot be accomplished to its maximum benefit. If the owner has not fully understood the processes to accomplish its goals, then how can anyone else in the organization. That's why much of the business coach's advice does not work. It is a constant insinuation technique delivered on media outlets that they hold the key to life and business. The truth is the person needs to create internal growth from foundational processes that identify opportunities at all levels of the business. Through an internal focus, you create an active position of innovation and development of capital.

Social media business coaches are so popular in today's age because they see an ever-growing need for people to be motivated. They know people don't understand financial variables, so they tug on the emotional aspect of business instead of the technical side.

As we're driven to work ourselves to the death to become successful, we lose ourselves in the work. We tell ourselves it's for a purpose, yet we're missing emotional intelligence.

The drive for success doesn't always come through success because the failures teach you so much about yourself and your abilities. It's important to not let the failures hold you back, no matter how crazy people think you are.

Dynasties don't always come with a playbook, but if you don't train yourself to be a constant learner, you won't reach your maximum potential. Maintaining a curious mindset allows you to develop new strategies over time. You're able to understand people at a deeper level because we're all searching for something we're missing in our life. It takes a greater sense of curiosity to create what is known as "grounded confidence."

Research continues to show small business owners fail because of cash flow, but no one is teaching people the right way to start a business. As small businesses need money, there are only a handful of criteria that are looked at, and if you don't fit the 9 percent "easy" qualifications, then you're out of luck. If they cannot get access to money and are not being guided to understand how to become bankable, then what chance do small business owners have?

Over time, the excitement of the business wears off, and the exhausting pressure of keeping everything together can weigh on our minds. Aspirations, lack of self-discipline, and lack of financial judgment from business concepts can keep us in a constant circle of dissatisfaction.

Ambition isn't enough to carry us through the hard times, and not building a system around financial analysis can be hard to access capital leading to business distress and lack of emotional stability.

CHAPTER 6

CURIOSITY
IS THE ENGINE
OF ACHIEVEMENT

———

One of the most important tools that can guard against economic failure for the small business is for the business owner to track the financial progress through financial statements and to analyze the effectiveness of the organization's governance of its profits. As Warren Buffet explains in his words, his craving for reading financial statements is the same as other men's desire to read *Playboy*.[85] What Warren Buffet, undeniably one of the greatest investors of all times, investigates is the opportunity to exploit the company's competitive advantage toward the market it serves.

---

85 Mary Buffett and David Clark, *Warren Buffett and the Interpretation of Financial Statements: The Search for the Company with a Durable Competitive Advantage,* Read by Karen White, Tantor Audio, December 1, 2008.

Before Price Arredondo was the director of business development, he was a business consultant and entrepreneur. His experience brings awareness to the needs of the owners, and he notices many of them don't really have an understanding of their financial numbers and are not even curious to know more. He expresses that even those who have accountants don't understand what it all means. The accountant keeps the books, and the business owner doesn't ask any questions to learn more. Most business owners only see their accountants at the end of the year and expect the accountant to reduce tax liability based on past data. These business owners don't use the expertise of professionals to learn more on how to do that through tax strategy and business processes. There must be an equal share in the responsibilities of making sure processes and procedures are up to date and being able to identify the gaps in the efficiency of the business.

Successful business owners like Warren Buffett study, plan, and forecast for future opportunities and possible adversities using their accountants and financial professionals to provide them as much data as possible to maximize profit and reduce taxes to maximize the use of the dollars gained.

This means owners like him study the business's financial history to find the consistencies in profit and look for any risk to the company's competitive advantage. There are different ways a company can produce an advantage over its competitors in the market. The easiest way to vacuum the most amount of cash into the business as often as possible can be the company's brand like Coca-Cola, or the even comparing financial strength of Geico, which allows Warren to create an investment strategy from all of the cash it makes from the "float." Float is the money the company receives from the monthly premiums received before claims need to be paid. This float allows Warren to invest in other businesses with a competitive advantage. He can accomplish this surplus of cash for a long period of time without having to change a thing because he's created a mechanism of returning money back from another source with his investment company in the middle.

I worked with a small business that is an excellent example of a business capitalizing on its competitive advantage. It was an oilfield equipment transportation company. They capitalized on their attention to safety and excellent customer service as leverage to negotiate with one of the largest oil and gas companies in the world. The owner's attention to safety was recognized month after month as one of the best transport companies to follow company standards. Their drivers were also expected to learn to abide by the same attention to safety protocols. This led to them assisting in training other equipment haulers on how to be as safe and efficient.

We used this as talking points to negotiate a commitment from the customer to use their services ahead of other transporters for a certain number of loads per week. Their agreement allowed the business to be financially supported so we could more aggressively approach new customers, add more revenue-producing assets, and introduce new products and services. The competitive advantage of this relationship allowed us to expand the business naturally. To understand how effective this strategy was, if you had invested ten thousand dollars at the beginning of the agreement, you could have made $327,000 after year five. For every one dollar invested, you would've made thirty-two dollars back.

It's a similar approach to Warren Buffett's investment strategy. If that strategy requires little or no effort on our part, so much the better. Securing a stable pipeline of work allowed us to attack the market effectively. We didn't get to that point by accident, either.

We studied and reviewed our financial position as often as possible, and when we made any decision, we looked at the financial impact it would have on the business advantage and the financial impact going forward. As we traveled, we would stay up late in the hotel room discussing our opportunities, issues with the business, how to fix them, and execution solutions so we could go after more rewarding opportunities.

Our drive was triggered to change the world. We would go over our hopes and dreams and what we would do once we escaped from the grasps of our meager upbringing. We didn't learn how to look at business this way from our parents or school. I learned by having a chance to work with a small business owner early in my career that shaped my business curiosity. His small business grew to sell for hundreds of millions of dollars. I was no longer there when he sold, but I learned a lot from working as their financial controller to help shape the policies and operational procedures early in the business's life cycle.

I learned from his educational discipline and his ambition, but what I learned the most was the difference between his approach to business and my father's approach. My grandma and grandpa, we called them Wella and Wello, immigrated to a small town in Texas with a population of less than a thousand people, and the largest employer was the railroad. My father didn't like school much. He was a class clown, and his family focused on labor more than education. Why not? The only opportunity for my father and his brothers and sisters to get an education was by joining the armed forces.

My father probably barely finished high school, and after he skated past graduation, he decided to go into the workforce. My dad has had many jobs throughout his life. My favorite was when he was a janitor for an elementary school when I was a kid. My favorite part was going to take him food or picking him up for work because he would let me play in the gym, where I won "tons" of NBA championships with the last-second shot. This was not the best time for the family financially, but I never knew any different because my family never made me feel like I was going without.

My dad, throughout his different pursuits, was always curious. He was very competitive and wanted to know as much about his job and the company as he could to do his best. He gained his business knowledge from asking questions and being interested in other people. He learned that for him, the best chance to get out of financial hardship and give my sisters and me a chance to live a better life and accomplish our own dreams was through owning his own business.

His business experience was from personal trial and error.

In reality, how much success was he expected to have?

My father didn't have anyone to show him the proper processes and controls, and slowly over time, his curiosity decreased, which led to the downturn of the business. If he could've understood at the time the importance of analyzing the financial data of the company, developing strategies from this data to position the company toward the best opportunities in the future, and building on his competitive advantage customer service and repair quality, industry awareness, and valuable vendor partnerships. Maybe it would've relieved the stress of it all by being more present and curious in his life, and maybe over the life of his business, he would've seen the traps he/we all fall into as business owners.

It wasn't until my first professional position working as a financial controller for a small oil and gas company that I observed how a well-structured business could be designed. With operational processes guided by financial trends, we would research explanations behind trends. If our analysis of the business seemed off, we would question why and dig deeper to make sure our processes were forward-looking, efficient, and took advantage of the future trends we predicted.

When I started with the company, we had six locations. We created processes to collect as much information from each location as possible to identify the habits of each location through their financial statements. This gave us an overall look at the economy by comparing the businesses in one region to ones in other regions. We also learned management's approach toward the overall mission to provide quality customer service and profitable vendor relationships through a strategic distribution channel to grow the company and constantly analyze variances to improve business performance.

This strategy created maximum profit and grew internal capital that was available to grow the business when the economy dropped, and many other businesses in our industry were failing. An opportunity for us as a company was to expand the company's reach and new business investments to improve the quality of work, grow the strength of the brand by reaching new areas of the US, and introduce new streams of income to better diversify the industries the company serves.

One way we took advantage of the economic downturn was to purchase failing businesses. The owner strategically looked for companies with the potential to increase revenue, but more importantly, improved the quality of work and strengthened the brand. One acquisition provided a better distribution into a new area of Texas, and it allowed the company to expand into a new market from primarily oil and gas into the industrial agricultural market. Another acquisition gave us an opportunity to distribute to the other side of Texas and introduced the company to municipality partnerships, and gave us access to projects in the public sector.

The owner created a competitive advantage through the relationships with vendors to make sure the partnerships were constantly profitable to maintain proper margins to manage growth. It was a different look at profitability than I had seen before. This wasn't something I saw my dad doing. It was a more strategic mindset from gathering as much information as possible to make the best decisions possible.

The owner showed his appreciation to everyone involved in the company. He saw the growth of the business as growth opportunities for the employees by maximizing the return on the company's capital and investing back into the people of the company.

There were so many people involved in the success of the business. So many people had to work together to create the success of the business. The owner's curiosity overflowed into every person in the company and to anyone outside that worked with the company.

One way he encouraged our curiosity was by giving management a monthly subscription from a motivational speaker's program that delivered challenging techniques to create positive action following our curiosity. The lessons I learned from these monthly exercises expanded my understanding of the management of my emotions and their importance for my success.

Curiosity was something my father had in common with the owner of this oil and gas company. It was emotional intelligence that separated the two. The owner of this company never stopped learning. He valued it so much he managed his day around it, which gave him a deeper purpose that guided how he ran the business, directed richer conversations with others, and encouraged more innovative solutions to any obstacles. He was given a sense of peace because his day was full of gathering and analyzing information, which he was able to use for better decision-making.

Unfortunately, my father fell into the trap of believing he was too busy to slow down. His mindset was on hustling, and he didn't take time to step back and analyze his purpose, his conversations with others, and identify the changes he needed to make to stabilize his growth both personally and professionally.

CHAPTER 7

CURIOSITY TAKES IGNORANCE SERIOUSLY

The decline in our desire to learn is affecting human society as a whole, but this characteristic is necessary for small business success. The incurious business owners focus on areas of the business that are not growth behaviors. They are focused on the lifestyle of what new money brings based on the desires they see in the media. The incurious business owners fall into the trap of thinking money will fix everything.

Their actions are not focused on creating a financial structure, doing research, and using innovation to avoid future dilemmas. For people like my dad, the financial system isn't made to make it. That's why to whom much is given, much is tested. It takes courage and curiosity to get out of the mental trap of not knowing how to make and keep money.

I saw this as a kid in my father, but the fatigue of business ownership continues to exist. It's a never-ending cycle of working hard.

The same habits that took my father down continue to exist, and as a small business community, we don't do enough to build each other up and mentor each other to promote the importance of education and its overall connection to a stable economy. There is an individualistic mindset that has taken over in the media, which is reflected in the sharing of misinformation within business owners.

As we've discussed, financial literacy is critical to fill in the gaps of uncertainty when dealing with the "back office" tasks. The back office is the portion of a company made up of administration and support personnel who are not client-facing. These are the administrative tasks most small business owners leave for the last.

It's the thing my dad said, "he didn't have time for." That's the trap. We feel so busy focusing on sales, marketing, and attracting customers that we're "too tired" to take care of the hard parts we don't like to deal with. We don't value the intangible aspects of running the business like:

- Separating ourselves from the business. Remove the emotional bond from the company by doing something enjoyable that clears the mind.
- Become familiar with unfamiliar parts of the business. Stay engaged in the activities of the business to understand the culture of the business and understand the processes to always maintain progressive systems.

- Improve relationships with others and widen our network. Connect with other people and build reliable relationships with both internal and external stakeholders. Relationships within the field create a larger resource to swap ideas and identify common opportunities.

One-on-one in-person training builds trust, motivation, self-efficacy, goal orientation, trust, interpersonal attraction, supervisory support, and feedback intervention.[86] The characteristics that build financial efficacy reveal positive effects of coaching, even as simple as finding someone whose positive actions you can mimic. Coaching can increase the clients' self-regulatory abilities and their job performance, but coaching is also effective in changing job attitudes, well-being, and coping abilities.[87]

I'm talking one-on-one with business professionals such as a CPA, small business development center, banker, attorney, or whoever you can meet that can fill any gaps of knowledge you may have. Not these online "self-made," make-you-rich-in-a-week, hustle-porn motivational speakers who are just a distraction from what's really going on in the small business owner's mind.

---

86 G. Bozer and Jones, R. J., "Understanding the factors that determine workplace coaching effectiveness: A systematic literature review," European Journal of Work and Organizational Psychology, 27(3), 342–361. doi :10.1080/1359432X.2018.1446946. (2018).

87 Carsten C. Schermuly and Carolin Graßmann, "A literature review on negative effects of coaching—what we know and what we need to know," Coaching: An International Journal of Theory, Research and Practice 12, no. 1 (2019): 39–66.

Of course, the "front office" tasks like sales and advertising are important. In the global market, the local corner store is competing with anyone connected to the web, but if you can't manage money when you don't have any, what's the chance you understand it when you start making it? So, the power of financial understanding falls into the hands of the accountants, software, and algorithms, and in return, we ignore small business financial efficacy in the illusion that if you save the owner time, the owner will be independent and free. It only creates more dependence on their services and reduces curiosity toward the "back office" tasks where the trends and weaknesses are revealed to gauge the "front office" activities to actually see what's working and what isn't.

As technology reveals new financial models, implementing and learning how to use financial tools are necessary to reduce business failure. Research continues to show business owners do not use these tools to make decisions. Entrepreneurs who produced financial statements more frequently had a higher probability of loan repayment and a lower probability to close their venture involuntarily. The truth is we need to create an internal strength from foundational processes to identify opportunities and goals for the "front office" to work more efficiently toward.

Successful business owners like Warren Buffett use financial models and ratios to reveal the competitive advantage of the company and structure the business so the "front office" can attack the money and the "back office" can protect it. In the beginning, we may have to do this ourselves, but in my experience, it's better to be a person like Warren and learn all aspects of the business to be able to see what areas need attention.

Have you ever watched the show *Shark Tank*? If you're anything like my family, we like to circle around the TV and watch the drama unfold as the Shark rips into the business owner for not understanding their business as savagely as if the episode was part of Shark Week.

Entrepreneurs are so impacted by their story they forget to understand their numbers and be ready for a rational explanation to validate them. People are looking to explain their hero journey to display their grit but forget about why they're on the show. Funding! You need to convince the investors you can create a return.

What good is the journey if you don't know the path, you can't explain how you got there, and you can't show how you'll sustain a profitable environment?

All the drive and ambition can't save us if we don't manage and secure our financial health. One reason curiosity is carried out by the most successful business owners is because it encourages perseverance over obstacles, achieving goals, and challenging themselves to develop enhanced skills. The mindset helps develop effort and focus on one's abilities to create solutions over obstacles that, at times, seem impossible to overcome.

A curious mindset allows us to overcome obstacles for the days when drive and ambition are running low. Using our curiosity to find solutions within our own business is critical.

While there are so many different components, strategies, and situations, I am going to focus on general information to give us a beginning.

UNDERSTANDING FINANCIAL STATEMENTS & RATIOS

Typically, small business owners provide these statements to decision-makers when they need lending and during tax time. However, these reports are very important in determining the stability of the company, highlighting opportunities, and identifying efficiencies and inefficiencies of the business operations, which is very important when working on strategy preparation.

The information from the administrative part of the business in the manner of accounting is necessary to capture all the financial data points to perform the analysis. "The primary function of accounting is to accumulate and communicate information essential to an understanding of the activities of an enterprise, whether large or small, corporate or non-corporate, profit or nonprofit, public or private."[88]

I have a unique view of business and business owners because of the different areas we work in, and I see a common theme within small businesses. They are only focused on reducing their tax liability, but when it comes to financing, they are slowed down by the fact that their accounting isn't up to date, and they need to get it together. When it comes to their taxes, many of them are not prepared for the CPA to do their taxes,

---

88 James J. Benjamin and Arthur J. Francia and Robert H. Strawser, Financial Accounting, (2015).

handing over a box of receipts and unfinished accounting records.

Leaving a wealth of knowledge lost because the business owner is not analyzing data consistently through the year. The amount of information you learn from accounting data is priceless because it is an inside look into the story of the day, month, quarter, etc. The accounting process generates reporting termed financial statements, and ratios and performance measures can be used to make financial decisions.

Financial statements summarize basic financial information and illustrate a business's story in numbers. The typical financial statements are the balance sheet, income statement, and cash flow statement. These reports are required in the financial decision-making process.

Balance Sheet. Provides information regarding the financial position of the business at a certain point in time. The information included in this report shows the assets, liabilities, and the owner's equity of the business.

ASSETS = LIABILITIES + OWNER'S EQUITY

Assets. The economic resources of the business to be used in the continuous operations of the business. These are things like cash, accounts receivable, equipment, land, buildings, and so on. When used properly, this area can increase the net worth of the business tremendously. This is what you can leverage as collateral to a lender to maximize the investment of the ownership.

Liabilities. Debts taken from a creditor against the assets of the business. Creditors and investors are concerned with the ability to pay the debt back. Use the debt to purchase assets that build the net worth of the business. My recommendation is to use debt only when necessary and never to fulfill expenses. This is the worst rate of return besides mismanaging the profits of the business. Acquire debt to purchase revenue-producing assets that could pay the debt back without relying on other areas to pay back. Over time as the debt is paid, it will increase the net worth and valuation of the business.

ASSETS – LIABILITIES = OWNER'S EQUITY

The liabilities are debt taken from a lender that are paid down over time and can be used to grow the business from purchase order financing to fulfill orders, asset-based lending. I've spoken with business owners who still do not like to take on debt, but I think if used properly, it can be a valuable tool to maximize the financial performance of the business. Too many people suggest offering equity to investors to fulfill growth or start a business. While there is a need for equity in some situations, for most small business owners with a good credit score and the right lending product, you can use the debt to purchase assets that assist in building the value of the business. Over time, this will build a relationship with your lender, and your lending capabilities can grow as long as you pay them back on time. Never use debt to fulfill expenses. This is the worst rate of return besides mismanaging the profits of the business.

DO YOU KNOW WHAT IT TAKES TO BE INVESTABLE SO YOU CAN ACCESS THE MONEY NEEDED?

Lenders want to give money to business owners, but too often, the business owner isn't prepared with credit, financial reports, or the collateral needed to get funding. Business owners are not reaching out to CPAs, bankers, investors, or other business owners to find out how to get access to capital.

Lenders look at what you're going to do with the money and if you've had a track record of a good return on your own profits.

ARE YOU GOING TO LET YOUR FRIEND BORROW MONEY WHEN HE HAS A HABIT OF NOT PAYING ANYONE BACK, AND HE'S ONLY GOING TO SPEND THE MONEY ON SOMETHING BAD FOR HIMSELF?

That's exactly how a lender will look at your business. Your credit score will show how well you've paid people in the past, your financial reports will show how profitable you are and if you create a good return with the profits you've made, and as you build assets for the company, the lender can see you're stable enough to maintain the assets you plan to purchase.

I've spoken with countless business owners who have great intentions but are not ready when they need money. One of the most important pieces to any business is financial reporting, and we continue to see business owners either do not have their financials prepared, or they are inaccurate.

Owners' Equity. Represents the claims the owners have against the net assets of the business. The Owners assume more risk than the creditors since the return on investment to the owners is not defined. Owners' equity of a business is normally divided by the source of equity, which is direct investments made by the owners and profits earned by the business.

There are certain legal differences associated with the different types of organizations.

Income Statement. The income statement, or operating statement, provides data as to the results of operations of the business for a specific period. Only transactions that affect revenues or expenses are categorized in the income statement. The results of the operations are determined by its revenues less expenses to result in the net income.

We can also look at the accounting equation, including the income statement results as:

ASSETS = LIABILITIES + OWNER'S EQUITY + (REVENUE – EXPENSES)

Mismanagement of the profits we won't be able to raise assets or capital to improve the equity in our business. Therefore, as we mentioned, we cannot manage our wants and desires and control our emotions to reduce the expenses and the loss of cash to grow the business. Mismanaging cash will result in a lack of organizational growth, as we see in the study performed by the Kelley School of Business at Indiana University. When a business creates uncertainty, there is bound to be a failure, and the aftermath of failure is often fraught with psychological, social, and further financial turmoil.

What caused my father to ultimately close his business was his customers were paying late, and he and my aunt, his business partner, and his "back office" did not follow up in time and it caused cash flow problems that triggered a snowball of problems he couldn't recover from. So, while the above equation makes sense without cash to pay the bills, it's hard to stay open.

RATIO ANALYSIS

Ratio analysis is a quantitative method of gaining insight into a company's liquidity, operational efficiency, and profitability by studying its financial statements such as the balance sheet and income statement. Investors and analysts employ ratio analysis to evaluate the financial health of companies by scrutinizing past and current financial statements. Comparative data can demonstrate how a company is performing over time and can be used to estimate likely future performance. Below are a few useful ratios.

Liquidity ratios. Measure a company's ability to pay off its short-term debts as they become due using the company's current or quick assets. Liquidity ratios include the current ratio, quick ratio, and working capital ratio.

CURRENT RATIO: CURRENT ASSETS / CURRENT LIABILITIES

Measures the capability of a business to meet its short-term obligations that are due within a year. It indicates the financial health of a company and how it can maximize the liquidity of its current assets to settle debt and payables.

QUICK RATIO: (CURRENT ASSETS – INVENTORY) / CURRENT LIABILITIES

Measures the ability of a business to pay its short-term liabilities by having assets that are readily convertible into cash. These assets are, namely, cash, marketable securities, and accounts receivable. These assets are known as "quick" assets since they can quickly be converted into cash.

Solvency ratios. Compare a company's debt levels with its assets, equity, and earnings to evaluate the likelihood of a company staying afloat over the long haul by paying off its long-term debt as well as the interest on its debt. Examples of solvency ratios include debt-equity ratios, debt-assets ratios, and interest coverage ratios.

DEBT-EQUITY RATIOS: (SHORT TERM DEBT + LONG TERM DEBT + OTHER FIXED PAYMENTS) / OWNERS EQUITY

Measures the weight of total debt and financial liabilities against total owners' equity. This ratio highlights how a company's capital structure is tilted either toward debt or equity financing.

DEBT-ASSETS RATIOS: (SHORT TERM DEBT + LONG TERM DEBT) / TOTAL ASSETS

Measures the percentage of assets that are being financed with debt. The higher the ratio, the greater the degree of leverage and financial risk. The debt to asset ratio is commonly used by creditors to determine the amount of debt in a company, the ability to repay its debt, and whether additional loans will be extended to the company. On the other hand, investors use the ratio to make sure the company is solvent, is able to meet current and future obligations, and can generate a return on their investment.

INTEREST COVERAGE RATIO:
Measures how well a company can pay the interest on its outstanding debts. The ICR is commonly used by lenders, creditors, and investors to determine the riskiness of lending capital to a company.

Profitability ratios. These ratios convey how well a company can generate profits from its operations: profit margin, return on assets, return on equity, return on capital employed, and gross margin ratios.

Return on Assets: Net Income / End of Period Assets

Measures how well a company is performing by comparing the profit (net income) it's generating to the capital it's invested in assets. The higher the return, the more productive and efficient management is in utilizing economic resources.

Return on Equity: Net Income / Owners Equity

Return on equity is a two-part ratio in its derivation because it brings together the income statement and the balance sheet, where net income or profit is compared to the shareholders' equity. Measures the total return on equity capital and shows the firm's ability to turn equity investments into profits. It measures the profits made for each dollar from owners' equity.

RETURN ON CAPITAL: NET OPERATING PROFIT AFTER TAX / INVESTED CAPITAL

Measures the percentage return that a company earns on invested capital. The ratio shows how efficiently a company is using the investors' funds to generate income.

Efficiency ratios. Evaluate how efficiently a company uses its assets and liabilities to generate sales and maximize profits. Key efficiency ratios include turnover ratio, inventory turnover, and days' sales in inventory.

TURNOVER RATIO: NET SALES / AVERAGE TOTAL ASSETS

Measures the efficiency with which a company uses its assets to produce sales. A company with a high asset turnover ratio operates more efficiently as compared to competitors with a lower ratio.

INVENTORY TURNOVER: COST OF GOODS SOLD / AVERAGE INVENTORY

Measures the number of times a business sells and replaces its stock of goods during a given period. A high inventory turnover generally means goods are sold faster, and a low turnover rate indicates weak sales and excess inventories, which may be challenging for a business.

ACCOUNTS RECEIVABLE TURNOVER: NET CREDIT SALES / AVERAGE ACCOUNTS RECEIVABLE

Measures how efficiently a company is collecting revenue—and by extension, how efficiently it is using its assets. The accounts receivable turnover ratio measures the number of times over a given period a company collects its average accounts receivable.

Understanding our financial position from the financial statements and ratios allows us to plan ahead and see the habits and trends of our business. Keeping financials and having a forward look toward the direction of our business allows us to see opportunities and prepare for unexpected obstacles. Take the phenomenon in 2020 where COVID-19 took so many people off-guard. There hasn't been an incident of its kind, but the businesses that survived and continued to do so found innovative ways to pivot into a new market, into a new partnership, and into new products and new designs. The time for innovation doesn't start when tragedy strikes but begins with planning and preparation on a continuous basis.

A 2018 study by the Routledge Taylor & Francis Group asked, "How do small business owners actually make their financial decisions?"[89] They looked to answer what the underlying factors are of financial decision-making based completely on the personal perspectives of the business owner.

---

89   Alexandra Wong, Scott Holmes, and Michael T. Schaper. "How do small business owners actually make their financial decisions? Understanding SME financial behaviour using a case-based approach," Small *Enterprise Research* 25, no. 1 (2018): 36–51.

They approach this study in two different ways: addressing the obstacles small businesses face when accessing external financing and the business owners' previous experiences and their perceptions on the ease of access to funding. The study provides a look into the financial circumstances small businesses face when they advance into new levels of growth.

Continue to invest in existing operations and focus on processes to identify key areas of efficiency and maximize the potential of cash flow, which will result in more opportunities for investment.

This is critical for small businesses to succeed in running. A consistently evolving business, through process improvement, will only continue to develop the business internally and maximize the return on competitive advantage.

Baruch Lev, professor at NYU, argues the usefulness of financial reporting is deteriorating. Surveys show financial executives are burdened by the preparation of financial statements versus the information they provide. As business owners see financial reporting as a daunting task only to be completed for taxes or lending, important strategic information is being ignored.

CHAPTER 8

CURIOSITY IS THE MOST IMPORTANT PART

―――

We can see through the achievements of Warren Buffet curiosity over the lifespan of a business can help assist in the reduction of business failure.

Why do we sell the lifestyle of the business and not the components like the policy makers, academics, scholars, and economists?

It's because humans are lazy, and they don't look for it. We'd rather have the cliff notes version in a thirty-second media feed. However, this causes us to get a watered-down version of what knowledge we can receive if we would read more and read material beneficial to our personal and business growth.

Business owners need to develop processes from curiosity by asking questions, listening to others, analyzing behavior, adjusting environmental influences, and challenging everything. A creative mindset of constant learning can overcome financial obstacles without the emotional rollercoaster from the fears and worries of not knowing something.

What causes us to lose the curious mindset we had when we started the business?

When we decide to start a business, we choose to take on the risks and difficulties that come along with it financially, administratively, and organizationally, especially when it comes to managing people. However, over time, failed businesses do not concentrate on the internal structure or invest in the intangibles of the business, such as culture, leadership, and open communication.

These characteristics are fostered effortlessly with a curious mindset. Results published in the *Harvard Business Review* from an interdisciplinary study performed by four professors from Bucknell University suggest when people work on "real" problems, this has a significant positive correlation with their long-standing conscientious motivation and curiosity.[90]

In this study, they define an entrepreneurial mindset using the three C's:

- **Curiosity**
- **Connection**
- **Value-Creation**

---

90 Margot A. Vigeant, M. Prince, K. Nottis, and A. Golightly, "Curious about student curiosity: Implications of pedagogical approach for students' mindset," Proceedings *of American Association for Engineering Education*, (2018).

This study accomplishes the linking of motivation and curiosity to show both how our desire to seek information stimulates motivation, and conscientious motivation is created by the knowledge learned. This motivation allows us to realize our intention of this newfound knowledge. The conscientious motivation gives our *why* and, more importantly, our curiosity shows us *how*.

We cannot deny the importance of motivation and curiosity in our success, yet we cannot measure them. That doesn't mean we don't wake up at three in the morning to listen to motivational speaker Eric Thomas yelling at you to "GRIND!" Therefore, we cannot deny the importance of certain components necessary to the business, even if there isn't a valuation for them yet. When the banks, investors, and policy makers create the financial model to value intangibles, they view as important, like environmental, social, and business control, we'll need to be prepared to understand these elements, like valuing a "motivated and prepared team."

The return of our intangible capital that investors and creditors pay attention to is not exchanged within the small business community. This is how we capitalize on our competitive advantage. We will look at several areas of intangible capital and how curiosity can help build tangible growth from an intangible strategy using:

- **Human Capital.** *Task motivation and optimism*
- **Information Capital.** *Efficacy and behavioral strategic sophistication*
- **Psychological Capital.** *Entrepreneurial intensity and resilience*

- *Social Capital.* *Hope and cognitive strategic sophistication*

The study from Bucknell University found companies that have successfully changed their strategies have needed only a small, limited number of behaviors to maximize the contributions of their people to the execution of their new strategies.[91]

When adopting change, this study proposes focusing on value creation in terms of behaviors that increase focus on customers, innovation, and results and focusing on strategy execution in the term of behaviors that increase employees' understanding of the company's mission, vision, and values.

Internal growth increases every aspect of the organization. Internal growth highlights human, informational, psychological, and social capital. These areas are needed to create a transformational business.

HUMAN CAPITAL. THE COMPANY CULTURE, TALENT, SKILLS, AND KNOWLEDGE OF THE EMPLOYEES.

Human motivation has been linked to curiosity as a source of development and emotional intelligence. Incorporating an inviting environment of cooperation and communication toward expected financial responsibilities produces an investment into human motivation that will help during financial hardships. However, losing interest over time can create a complacent mindset and lead to financial distress

---

91   Robert S. Kaplan, and David P. Norton, "Measuring the strategic readiness of intangible assets," Harvard *business review* 82, no. 2 (2004): 52–63.

because it leads to a reactive approach to problem-solving. A curious mindset can increase the chance of creativity to develop solutions and find reliable opportunities for growth.

I have a friend, Chef Alejandro Barrientos—there aren't enough titles for this guy—who is first and foremost a philanthropist in our hometown. He's also been on one of my family's favorite shows, *Beat Bobby Flay*. He's a James Beard award-winning chef, so when I get any chance to cook with him, I do. I've always admired his food as a customer and now was my chance to talk to him about his business mind. I got to use the excuse of interviewing him for the chance to chill with a pro. I was blown away by his story and his conviction to pass on knowledge to other restaurateurs. When we spoke, COVID-19 had just swept through the world, and he was learning a new way of running his burger joint along with millions of other people in the industry.

His major lessons centered around his love for people and bringing them together through his food. At the time, he said for businesses to be successful in any industry, you have to be creative, train your team right, and get out of the way. Chef Alejandro sees going through his trials and adversity early in his career as motivation to advise others and make their path easier than his. He attributes his success to everyone around him: to his brother for motivating him to start culinary school, to his wife for supporting him even when his passion wasn't bringing in money, to his teachers and mentors he learned from, and to his team for challenging him and always supporting his dreams.

One of the most unique stories that demonstrated his invest-ment in the human capital around him was he has a different team member come up with a menu item and go through the process from developing the burger, to pricing the cost, to marketing it. If the burger did well, it would stay on the menu, and he would share profits with the team member. During the practice, each member of the team grows to understand the importance of every step of the business, and it unifies the team.

This was a lesson Chef Alejandro took from his time as an instructor at the local community college. He noticed the classes most important to the students were the classes they would "space out" on, which were *the business classes.* Does this sound familiar? It should. For most of us, we seem to lose focus on anything that takes too much effort.

With the mindset that I'll just hustle harder and money will solve the problem causes problems for our future self because we are not prepared to make better decisions in the future. When we as business owners are focused on the money, we lose sight of the intangible like the people around us.

Chef Alejandro attributes his success and peace of mind to the people around him, and after our conversation, it was obvious why he's a celebrity—*his love for people is infectious.*

Chef Alejandro created a culture in his business based on human capital to enhance creative problem-solving. Cre-ative problem-solving occurs when employees challenge and cross-pollinate existing knowledge and approaches with new ideas.[92] Research demonstrates framing work around learning goals (e.g., skill development) rather than performance goals (e.g., hitting targets) boosts motivation. Those motivated by learning goals tend to acquire a greater diversity of skills, do better in problem-solving, and log better work performance, although organizations generally prioritize performance goals, according to Harvard behavioral scientist Francesca Gino.[93] Leaders can counteract this trend by advocating for the importance of learning and by rewarding people both for their performance and for the learning needed to get there.

According to the 2011 study published by *The Journal of Psychology*, "Research in applied psychology and strategic human resource management clearly indicates that investing in human capital can yield positive individual as well as organization-level performance outcomes."[94] The article goes on to

92 Francesca Gino, "The business case for curiosity," Harvard *Business Review* 96, no. 5 (2018): 48–57.

93 Ibid

94 B. E. Becker & M. A. Huselid, Strategic human resource management: Where do we go from here? *Journal of Management,32*, 898–925. (2006). doi:10.1177/0149206306293668. ; D. E. Bowen & C. Ostroff, Understanding HRM firm performance linkages: The role of "strength" of the HRM system, *Academy of Management Review, 29*, 203–221. (2004). doi:10.2307/20159029. ; M. A. Huselid, The impact of human resource management practices on turnover, productivity, and corporate financial performance, *Academy of Management Journal, 38*, 635–672. (1995). doi:10.2307/256741. ; Le, H., Oh, I. S., Shaffer, J., & F. Schmidt, Implications of methodological advances for the practice of personnel selection: How practitioners benefit from meta-analysis, *Academy of Management Perspectives,* (2007).21, 6–15. ; M. Subramony, N. Krause, Norton, J., & Burns, G. N. The relationship between human resource investments and organizational performance: A firm-level examination of equilibrium theory. *Journal of Applied Psychology. 93,* (2008). 778–788. doi:10.1037/0021-9010.93.4.778.

explain through investing in human capital, the business owner can protect their competitive advantage by using resources to enhance the knowledge of the people behind the business and the progress of processes and performance that competitors cannot replicate, reinforcing a competitive advantage.

Furthermore, human capital is unique and cannot be replicated because of our own unique perspective on life, and investments in training designed to build human capital influences performance.[95] Taken together, including the experiences, education, and training, have consistently been viewed as central drivers of strategy and performance.[96] The culture in our business is influenced by the emotions, experiences, personal investment in knowledge from all of the people involved in the business to perform well.

A strategic daily life through curiosity is found by training your thoughts and training your habits, leading to positive action toward and training others. What good is it to be an owner that ignores their people until it's convenient for them? We need to seek other people's advice because we genuinely value their opinion. Chef Alejandro makes sure to teach all of his team different aspects of the business to keep everyone interested because he values the advice he receives from them.

95 Combs, J., Liu, Y., Hall, A., & D. Ketchen, (2006). How much do high-performance work practices matter? A meta-analysis of their effects on organizational performance, *Personnel Psychology, 59,* 501–528. doi:10.1111/j.1744-6570.2006.00045.x.

96 K. Andrews, *The concept of corporate strategy,* Homewood, IL: Dow Jones–Irwin. (1965).; A. D. Chandler, *Strategy and structure: Chapters in the history of American industrial enterprise,* London, England: MIT Press. (1962).; Hambrick, D. C., & Mason, P. A. (1984). Upper echelons: The organization as a reflection of its top managers. *Academy of Management Review, 9,* 193–206. doi:10.2307/258434.

This gives him a competitive advantage because it keeps his menu fresh and his operations unique to the chef's personal and professional strategy. Another driver highlighted by *The Journal of Psychology* and adopted in Chef Alejandro's culture is that a firm-specific human capital, in contrast, is valuable because it helps employees make decisions congruent with a firm's unique strategy, organizational context, and competitive environment.[97]

Human capital allows the employees to enhance and explore their position to create the most opportunities for growth or efficiencies in the business.

1. Focus is on process improvement
2. Educational improvement
3. Emotional improvement

INFORMATION CAPITAL. THE COMPANY TECHNOLOGY, INNOVATION, AND PROCESS OF DATA.

"[Warren] expends a lot of energy checking out details and ferreting out nuggets of information, way beyond the balance sheet. He would go back and look at the company's history in-depth for decades. He used to pay people to attend shareholder meetings and ask questions for him. He checked out the personal lives of people who ran companies he invested in. He wanted to know about their financial status, their personal habits, what motivated them. He behaves like an investigative journalist. All this stuff about

---

97 Y. Kor & J. T. Mahoney, (2005). How dynamics, management, and governance of resource deployments influence firm-level performance, *Strategic Management Journal, 26,* 489–496. doi:10.1002/smj.459.

flipping through Moody's Manual's picking stocks, it was a screen for him, but he didn't stop there."[98]

Jathan Sadowski in 2019 publicized in *Big Data & Society* that the collection of data is now a central element of increasingly more sectors of contemporary capitalism. He goes on to show the importance of data collection by saying, "The imperative to capture all data, from all sources, by any means possible influences many key decisions about business models, political governance, and technological development."[99]

Just as we expect corporations to be profit-driven, we should expect small businesses to be data-driven. That is, data propels new ways of doing business and governance.

Warren Buffett notoriously builds his curiosity by reading half a day, every day. He has been quoted saying, "My policy [is] reading every annual report in sight that can further my knowledge about anything."[100]

Data capital allows the business to identify and capture all data to make better decisions. As small businesses continue to fail for the same reason over and over, year after year, it is very important to understand how technology can create efficiencies in our processes and monitoring.

---

98 "Staying Curious, "Investment Masters Class," (Investment Blog), June 28, 2018, accessed October 22,2020.

99 Jathan Sadowski, "When data is capital: Datafication, accumulation, and extraction," Big Data & Society 6, no. 1 (2019): 2053951718820549.

100 Kathleen Elkins, "Berkshire Hathaway star followed Warren Buffett's advice: Read 500 pages a day," Make it(blog), March 27, 2018.

Owners do not focus on data because it identifies problems with the business, and the owner is too intimately connected with the business and cannot accept they may have created something they can't fix. Instead of breaking down the processes and taking the time to evaluate all scenarios of the problem, the business owner doles out the old, tired saying, "time is money." Yes, time is money, but spending less time on a problem does not resolve the fact that the issue will continue to happen. Without creating a sustainable process, the issue will come up again and again, costing more in the end.

Another area that causes problems when not capturing complete data is this creates a gluttony of misinformation throughout the company, and ultimately the business owner is making decisions based on incomplete data.

Psychological Capital. The leadership and organizational behavior.

Happiness doesn't show up where you thought it would. It is through accomplishments and using our unique abilities to accomplish these goals that happiness is found. It is through the challenges of building the business from setting policies, to operational processes, to knowing and protecting your competitive advantage. Happiness comes from possessing a unique set of skills that no one has because it comes from our experiences and growing emotionally to guard your future.

This is an understanding of who we are, an inner reflection in understanding our purpose. PsyCap draws from positive psychology in general and positive organizational behavior (POB) in particular. The first-order positive psychological resources that make up PsyCap include hope, efficacy, resilience, and optimism—or the HERO within.[101]

What do you want to do every day and *why*? Incorporating curiosity with a positive mindset helps us to find *how* to execute our *why*. A curious mindset puts first the importance of self-reflection and building relationships.

A curious mindset constructs an awareness of the importance of growth and awareness of our unique strengths. When we are confident in our skills, we can build an organization to prepare for economic turmoil through team development, a positive mindset, and the desire to want to know-how. When we don't create a mindset of curiosity, we lose the team to instability and decreased performance which enhances the risk of failure.

When we learn to establish mastery, ask questions to learn from others, and create and execute positively on tasks toward our goals, we are using our curiosity. Curiosity is one way we can create a "positive motivational strategy" toward running the business. This positive emotional state is the motivation we need to overcome obstacles and keep the passion like it was the first day in the business.

In a 2017 study, the University of Nebraska-Lincoln defined psychological capital, or PsyCap for short, as an individual's positive psychological state of development that is characterized by:

---

101 Fred Luthans and Carolyn M. Youssef-Morgan, "Psychological capital: An evidence-based positive approach," Annual *review of organizational psychology and organizational behavior* 4 (2017): 339–366.

Having confidence (efficacy). Take on and put in the necessary effort to succeed at challenging tasks. Efficacy is defined as "the individual's conviction or confidence about his or her abilities to mobilize the motivation, cognitive resources, or courses of action needed to successfully execute a specific task within a given context."[102]

Making a positive attribution (optimism). Positive mindset toward succeeding now and in the future. Optimism is a positive explanatory style that attributes positive events to personal, permanent, and pervasive causes and interprets negative events in terms of external, temporary, and situation-specific factors.

Persevering toward goals and, when necessary, redirecting paths to goals (hope). Hope is defined as "a positive motivational state based on an interactively derived sense of successful (a) agency (goal-directed energy) and (b) pathways (planning to meet goals)."[103] On the basis of this definition, hope includes two key dimensions: agency, which is the willpower or determination to pursue goals, and pathways, which is the "waypower" or ability to generate alternative paths to achieve goals when obstacles hinder plans.

When beset by problems and adversity, sustaining and bouncing back and even beyond to obtain success

102 AD Stajkovic, F. Luthans, 1998b, Social cognitive theory and self-efficacy: Going beyond traditional motivational and behavioral approaches, *Organ. Dyn.* 26:62–74.

103 CR Snyder, L Irving, Anderson J., 1991, Hope and health: Measuring the will and the ways. In *Handbook of Social and Clinical Psychology*, ed. CR Snyder, DR Forsyth, pp. 285–305. Elmsford, NY: Pergamon.

(resilience). Resilience is defined as "the capacity to rebound or bounce back from adversity, conflict, failure, or even positive events, progress, and increased responsibility."[104]

The development of our thoughts and how we choose to live our life affects the way we manage and run our business. This is what most failed business owners lose sight of. Our personal thoughts and actions make up our business decision-making.

Our actions should be aimed toward something meaningful, enthusiastic, and helpful to our future selves. We can obtain hope, efficacy, resilience, and optimism in several different ways and all are connected to our curiosity.

The University of Nebraska-Lincoln introduces ways to accomplish these key areas in our life and can be very useful in our business decision-making.

Hope. Our *"waypower" is* our ability to create alternative paths to accomplish goals when obstacles present themselves to us. Hope is a positive emotional state based on activity toward actionable tasks and a plan to reach them. This is our *"willpower,"* or our determination to pursue goals.

Efficacy. Our conviction or confidence in our own ability to successfully execute tasks toward a specific goal. There are four specific ways we can develop our efficacy:

---

104 F. Luthans, 2002b, Positive organizational behavior: Developing and managing psychological strengths, *Acad. Manag. Exec.,* 16(1):57–72.

- Mastery or success experiences
- Vicarious learning or modeling the behavior of someone positive
- Positive social feedback and social influence
- Physical and mental curiosity toward positive actions

Resilience. Our ability to bounce back from adversity, conflict, failure, or even positive events to progress and increase responsibility. This comes from consistency and practice. Resilience comes from patterns and processes to overcome emotional peaks and valleys. More importantly, the awareness of reducing risk by utilizing personal, social, and psychological resources.

Optimism. Our positive style precedes positive actions for personal, permanent, and purposeful motives. It is important to practice our optimism and positivity because it is also linked to how we observe negative experiences, whether they be external, temporary, or situation-specific.[105]

You might be asking yourself, *How much more do I have to worry about when I have to be out there making money?*

Now I must work even harder to make space to work on these things. These are things we can work on throughout the day without much effort, especially to overcome the days when you'd rather be in bed under the covers.

This can be achieved by just picking up the phone and listening to the other person, having a coffee with someone

---

105 Seligman MEP, 1998, *Learned Optimism*, New York: Pocket Books.

you treasure, researching something toward mastering your passion, or joining a group of like-minded people to provide a positive impact for others. I have days I want to escape, but I've surrounded myself around people who elevate my confidence, positively challenge my ideas, and follow me with actions.

What I've learned over the years is I need to be around people who challenge my curiosity to generate positive mental actions of hope and optimism. Curiosity remains a key characteristic in my daily life, and it has led me to better decision-making, overcoming my fears, developing empathy, and becoming more self-aware.

Social Capital. The company relates to economic development and social responsibilities.

Social Capital creates a true desire to learn who others are. What is their story? We become so ingrained in what our meaning is. Creating a network of people around you can help challenge and develop us as a leader and creates a desire to help others more.

James Bishop said about people coming to him way too late, James is a wealth manager for business owners, and he sees that business owners don't always see the value in preparedness so they don't seek his advice until now the business owner has to catch up on retirement, legacy planning, succession planning.

Mr. Bishop expressed most business owners who come to him in developing a retirement strategy, exit plan, and so on are already five years too late. By the time the business owner has decided to focus on retirement, it's now even harder and more sacrifices are needed.

He states most business owners are not curious enough to look toward their long-term goals and get lost in the business. They cannot answer questions like:

- What are your passions?
- What do you like to do?
- Do you want to fish, or do you like to golf?
- Is there some philanthropy or some other meaningful thing that you like to do?
- Do you like to travel, or do you have any grandchildren?

Most business owners are so focused on the hustle of the now that we lose our long-term focus and curiosity of the moment. We don't see ourselves in the future because we are so focused on getting today right. There are ways to get past this, and researchers have discovered two levels of curiosity:

Perception-directed curiosity—focuses on an individual's attention to objects in one's immediate environment.

Knowledge-driven curiosity—refers to one's desire for information and knowledge.

Knowledge-driven curiosity creates an exploratory behavior to decision-making and forward-thinking mindset that helps us plan for the future.

There is evidence to support the theory that a new reporting system is needed to strengthen small businesses, and it will financially progress into the new technological era. This can only be accomplished by establishing a reason to include intangibles into the business valuation process by including new reporting models that offer present-day indicators to support the improvement of patterns that promote financial safeguards.

I've worked with business owners who change their goals daily based on their bank balance. When we don't create a mindset of curiosity, we lose the development of the team to build stability and maximum performance that reduces the risk of failure.

CHAPTER 9

INTANGIBLE IS THE SEED OF THE TANGIBLE

There is evidence that intangible assets can provide a greater net worth to the business than what is perceived by the common business owner. Imagine trying to put a value on something that cannot be touched or seen, like how the intangible of curiosity can help us find an inner intimacy in our personal lives. Intangibles can have the same impact on our businesses. Areas we cannot see are hard to put our focus on every single day because it takes constant effort that, as humans, we are just not capable of. However, when our personal ambition and drive are no longer enough to reach our maximum potential, our curiosity and the search for the truth will carry us the rest of the way.

I like going to small bookstores to find old financial books. I enjoy reading the practices and how they have evolved over the centuries. I picked up a financial accounting book from 1975, and, to my surprise, there wasn't anything in the book about it.

An intangible asset is an asset not physical in nature, such as brand recognition, organizational processes, financial sustainability, the talent of the team, and intellectual property like patents, copyrights, and trademarks. According to Investopedia:

- Intangible assets can be considered indefinite (a brand name, for example) or definite, like a legal agreement or contract.
- Intangible assets created by a company do not appear on the balance sheet and have no recorded book value.[106]

This is where you find your competitive advantage. The creation of brand recognition like Coca-Cola has done is the stuff of legends. The amount of money they've made purely on the name itself is mind-boggling. This is what intrigues investors, like Warren Buffett, to invest in the companies they do. What is that intangible that separates this company from any other, something your competitor cannot replicate?

Just like our own curiosities, our businesses need to reflect who we are, who we want to be, and more importantly, they need to be unique. We all have obstacles and weaknesses. This goes for our businesses as well. We must be aware weaknesses will always be present because "new levels bring new devils." This is why these phony business coaches make so much money. They prey on the vulnerable and lost people who get paranoid at every new level.

---

106 "Intangible Asset," Investopedia, accessed February 27, 2021.

If we know and protect our competitive advantage, we wouldn't need basic psychological sales training to get you motivated toward action. You'll be making money, which makes any human move. It's no different in our personal lives. If we accept and protect our uniqueness, then we won't be fooled by other flawed humans telling us what we should be or not be, and we will stop worrying about the financial ups and downs and focus on creating a competitive advantage.

As we see with Coca-Cola, they don't even have to change to be successful. They won! As a matter of fact, people were outraged when they announced they were going to change the recipe. According to their website, "When the announcement of the return of 'old' Coca-Cola was made in July 1985, those hoarding as many as 900 bottles in their basements could stop their self-imposed rationing and begin to drink the product as they always had—as often as they'd like."

That July day, the story that the "old" Coca-Cola was returning to store shelves as Coca-Cola classic led two network newscasts and made the front page of virtually every major newspaper. Consumers applauded the decision. Just two days after the announcement of Coca-Cola classic, The Coca-Cola Company had received 31,600 telephone calls on their hotline. Coca-Cola was obviously more than just a soft drink. The events of 1985 forever changed the dynamics of the soft drink industry, and the success of The Coca-Cola Company, as the Coca-Cola brand soared to new heights and consumers continued to remember the love they have for Coca-Cola.[107] They won!

Warren Buffett tells this story of selling pop at seven years old in Omaha. He noticed in the summertime, everyone would go outside and have a soda and enjoy the weather because they didn't have air conditioning, and the soda was cold. He had the curiosity to go around and collect all of the bottle caps around the neighboring gas stations. At the time, they only sold bottles, and on the side of the cooler was a bottle opener, and you could open your bottle, and the caps would fall in a small container. He collected about eight thousand bottle caps and saw there was an overwhelming amount of Coca-Cola caps. So, he decided he'd sell Coke.

I love this story because it shows his curiosity to research what people were drinking so he knew what they would buy. He took the time to find people's behaviors to reduce his risk. In a 2015 interview, Warren was asked, "What excites you these days in technology, innovation, and new businesses?" He replies by holding a Coke can up and saying, "This one. I'm the kind of guy that likes to bet on a sure thing. Since 1886, you can see year over year the consumer drinks more, to where we're serving 1.8 billion 8 ounce servings a day."[108]

107   "The Story of One of the Most Memorable Marketing Blunders Ever: The History of New Coke," Coca-Cola, Accessed February 19, 2021.

108   The Coca-Cola Company, "Warren Buffett on Why He'll Never Sell a Share of Coke Stock," Coca-Cola 2013 Annual Shareowners meeting, YouTube video, :48, https://youtu.be/4p1_5bZ8I4M.

He continues on to say, "I like wonderful brands. You must take care of them, but if you take care of a great brand, it's forever."[109]

According to Baruch Lev of the Philip Bardes Professor of Accounting and Finance at New York University's Stern School of Business, current financial statements provide very little information about the influence intangibles, like branding, have on tangible assets. Even worse, much of the information provided is partial, inconsistent, and confusing, leading to significant costs to companies, to investors, and to society as a whole.

In his article "Remarks on the Measurement, Valuation, and Reporting of Intangible Assets." Baruch argues this new technological age of "creative workers," investments in research and development, brand development, and software are being undervalued in the overall measurement of the investment of a company.[110]

Baruch Lev explains financial reports have become useless because of the inaccuracies of financial data, and this issue provides further evidence small business owners must focus on their organizational structure. Small businesses that typically fail do not have processes to identify inaccuracies in their organization. So, they manage their business by the checkbook. If they do not implement functions to support growth and create forwarding looking opportunities, an economic shift can result in the small business losing its

---

109 Ibid
110 Baruch Lev, "Remarks on the measurement, valuation, and reporting of intangible assets," (2003).

placement in the capital marketplace. That's why I say, "good positions don't create stability; good moves do." If you are aware of your competitive advantage, you can shift in uncertain times.

We must shift our concentration toward improving the obstacles facing small businesses through transparent terms using traditional methods. We will explore the forms of intangible capital that we must focus on to strategically protect our competitive advantage. Baruch Lev's theory provides a platform for expanding the current system of financial reporting for small businesses.

Inaccuracies in financial statements affect the cash flow in small businesses much more dramatically. For example, financial statements frequently get ignored in small businesses because there isn't an emphasis placed on the importance of analyzing company data. For some, financial reporting and accounting seem too complex and unexciting, so the business owner delays entering transactions and, in return, misses out on understanding the habits and trends of the business.

It is in our reporting that we validate the story of investors, lenders, and other examiners of our financial behavior. This provides a snapshot of our efforts in running the operations of our business. It shows how we've made money, how we've spent money, and how we've managed our money. We can use our financials as leverage to assist in the growth of our business, in pointing out the flaws in our processes, and the execution of our money management with all the benefits of creating financial statements.

So why do many small business owners only prepare them when they're getting a loan or doing taxes?

This is because intangibles are not valued correctly in the current accounting methods. So, business owners tend to ignore them when there is no recognition. Furthermore, there is no disclosure needed for the small business owner to describe the effects of their intangible assets.

For example, in France, companies are required to disclose "innovation revenues," those revenues that come from recently introduced products, so they can track the efficiency of the companies' ability to innovate and take the product to market.

According to Baruch, several studies by French economists have shown this information is very valuable in predicting the future growth and productivity of companies. Reporting like this can better help in understanding more clearly how to gauge our businesses better.

While much work is being done by the Financial Accounting Standards Board (FASB) as well as corporate CEOs, accountants from large accounting firms, and other corporate professionals, these conversations are not being dispersed down to the little guys. We are left trying to figure out the new methods of thought until these regulations and policies are implemented.

Investigation into understanding the behavior of small business owners has been increasing, and studies show accounting-based information in decisions is decreasing. The accounting-based decisions we make now are based on the purchasing power of the business and overlooks the importance of the intangibles of running a business, i.e., employee training, technology, and research and development. Systematically, Baruch's study found businesses that invested more heavily in research and development, much like curiosity, provided these companies with four times the gains than their competitors strictly because of the knowledge gained. Finding a research and development categorization in a small business is like finding a needle in a haystack. Small businesses do not invest in research and development.

The emotional attachment of "where to spend the money?" eliminates the need to conduct further research into the company. The lack of attention to the intangible aspects of the business, such as research, has created an ever-increasing gap between small businesses and innovation. *Harvard Business Review* performed a study that showed "a significant difference between the success and failure of small firms, and the common theme is an investment in the intangibles. The research expands to describe the growth opportunities for small businesses are shrinking, and the nimbleness and grit are increasingly under pressure."[111] Smaller companies are becoming more vulnerable to external dangers, but an investment in the internal factors—the intangible—can minimize the threat of hardships."

---

111 Vijay Govindarajan, Baruch Lev, Anup Srivastava, and Luminita Enache, Harvard Business Review. "The Gap Between Large and Small Companies Is Growing. Why?" August 16, 2019, https://hbr.org/2019/08/the-gap-between-large-and-small-companies-is-growing-why.

This seems to be an overall understatement in the value of intangibles all over the world, not just in the US but in Europe, Australia, and Malaysia, with individual studies coming up with the same conclusion: intangibles are increasing in importance, and a valuation needs to be seriously considered to reflect the current knowledge-based economy. As reported by *The Journal of Intellectual Capital,* findings reveal the Malaysian market developed intangible assets with significant development from 2004 onward. It also reveals the book value of net assets is declining as greater interest has now been developed in employing intangible assets and earnings as important variables.

Intangible assets are important strategic corporate assets, which are either ignored or not managed. These assets include brand name, research and development, human capital, customers' database, technology, and innovation.

In the new knowledge economy, managing tangible assets alone is not sufficient. There is a need for Malaysian companies to also focus on intangible assets to improve their competitive advantage.[112]

Undervaluation means the cost of capital of these companies, as well as emerging market economies, is excessive; it is more difficult for these firms to finance research and development and other investments that create intangible assets.[113] In the

---

112 Norhana Salamudin, Ridzwan Bakar, Muhd Kamil Ibrahim, and Faridah Haji Hassan, "Intangible assets valuation in the Malaysian capital market," Journal *of Intellectual Capital* (2010).

113 Baruch Lev, "Remarks on the measurement, valuation, and reporting of intangible assets," (2003).

next chapter, we will go over in a little more detail some ways to create an impactful focus on the intangibles of the business.

CHAPTER 10

THE VALUE OF CURIOSITY IS TO USE IT

———

How do we benefit from curiosity when we've distorted our view of human development with the goal of a glamorous lifestyle? Once we feel like there's no gap between what we know and what we want to know, we stop learning.

I recently spoke with the director of an entrepreneur incubator, Michael Crain. His primary purpose is to lead aspiring business owners to the necessary resources needed to start a business, such as business plans and financing. He stated the most common problem he finds is when someone wants to start a business, they don't fully understand the process until they're "in too deep."

Michael Crain said the most common reason why aspiring entrepreneurs need to rely on the pay-for-success model is that they have not done the research on the product, the industry, and they've invested a lot of time and money on a product that doesn't fit the market they're trying to serve.

"Research, research, research is what I find as the acute problem," Crain mentions. In his study, he found there is a 70 percent chance of failure before start-up because of the following reasons:

1. *They develop a product that doesn't fit the market.*
2. *They don't understand their target audience because they believe everyone will buy their product because it's a million-dollar idea.*
3. *They recognize their target audience, but they don't know the distribution channels to get to their audience.*
4. *They assume variables that don't exist, thinking something will happen in the future without any proof.*

Much of the reason is people don't have a stable financial background, to begin with. Mr. Crain said, "I'll be honest, this was me. I jumped in feet first, starting a manufacturing company with the mentality that no matter what, I was going to survive." He attributes this to his youth growing up in Compton and his father's advice.

Crain credits his intuition to the streets of Compton, and he uses his "street smarts" to support his academic approach to assisting start-ups. When I asked Mr. Crain what he recommends to start-ups in his program, he replied he challenges their curiosity to do their own research to strengthen their position.

If not, at some point, their luck will run out. If they're not capable of understanding how to manage their business and are not curious enough to learn, they increase their chances of failure. You can start with the school of hard knocks, but you need to be a student of the game. Continue to learn, and expand on the skills that got you to this point to maintain a flexible financial position in the business. It's no different on the block or in business. If you're not prepared, you will succumb to the pressure from those who are.

To someone who is not prepared, every opportunity to make money seems like the next deal of a lifetime when you're broke and ambitious. In the inception phase of the business, there aren't set structures and "ways of doing things," we just need to find a way to get things done. However, at this phase of the business, attention needs to be placed on systems and controls and planning for the next phase of the business.

I have been fascinated by the success of Warren Buffet. He has been listed as one of the richest persons in the world and has achieved so much with a type of laid-back honesty and a strong desire to learn. Warren has attributed much of his growth to his development of a curious mindset. He has recognized his strong desire to read everything in sight as his superpower to create ideas, learn from others, and create opportunities. Curiosity is a motivator for learning, influential in decision-making, and crucial for healthy mental development. Much of the reason curiosity is not studied more is because the broad definition is closely linked to creativity in child development, so as adults, we ignore the expansion of creativity and replace it with what we believe to be truthfulness.

The study of curiosity has not been around for long. Much of the early research for curiosity was thought to be that organisms are only curious during times of hunger or thirst. It is now more commonly understood that there are other times when our curiosity is provoked. It is further hypothesized that curiosity about a topic will not be invoked when either there are no information gaps identified or if the individual feels they already know the information. In addition, it is suggested curiosity becomes stronger the closer the individual feels they are to achieving the knowledge, and there is a pleasant feeling of satisfaction when information gaps are resolved.[114]

In the US education system, which is now heavily focused on students meeting fixed standards and performing well on standardized tests, curiosity can actually create a type of risk for teachers insofar as it threatens performance toward these rigid goals.[115] As adults, we need to spark our curiosity past what we've been taught. As business owners, it is necessary we:

1. Create work environments most likely to spark curiosity to help create solutions to business uncertainty.
2. Help employees by encouraging curious behavior.

114 Celeste Kidd and Benjamin Y. Hayden, "The psychology and neuroscience of curiosity," Neuron 88, no. 3 (2015): 449–460.

115 S. Engel, "The case for curiosity," Educational Leadership, 70(5):3640, 2013.

CONCLUSION

———

I remember jumping into the bed with my dad one morning before church as he read the Sunday paper. He had excitement and curiosity on his face after reading an article that offered training into a new and developing world of business: the technology business, his next million-dollar idea. My father didn't have someone to show him how to manage the business, so his curiosity had to carry him through the challenging times of starting his business.

Over the next several months, he would travel for training to repair copiers, printers, and fax machines. At the time he started, it was an innovative business, and there wasn't much competition. Over the years, my dad built a reputation for wonderful customer support and service, so much so he was the leading repairman in the area and landed a major contract, which was a fifteen-floor building with one of the premier oil and gas companies in the industry.

I can still remember the feeling of walking into my dad's office. He had a little window you had to pass that opened into my cousin's office as the secretary. When you turned around the corner, it opened into my dad's workshop, where he kept his supplies and inventory. In the middle was a large worktable where he would fix the repairs that couldn't be fixed quickly in the client's office.

He worked late nights, early mornings and did whatever it took to get the job done. I got to see the inside of the business at a young age, and I experienced how emotional the business can cause a person to be. As I worked with my consulting clients, I noticed every business owner carries fears and anxieties, and it wasn't any different than what I saw my father going through.

It's a creation we build with our blood, sweat, and tears, but for many, it causes a burden on them and their family. For most of the time he owned the business, I just wanted my dad to be around. His aspirations, self-discipline, and lack of financial judgment from business concepts kept him in a constant circle of dissatisfaction. Like other dads, he was trying his best to give me a better life than he had. What neither of us knew at the time was we weren't prepared to understand what we were really up against. A financial curse and emotional vulnerability passed on generationally in his family, and it's something I must still be mindful of today in my own life.

Hope, Efficacy, Resilience, and Optimism

I read a quote once that has always stayed with me. Spanish philosopher George Santayana is credited with saying, "Those who cannot remember the past are condemned to repeat it." I spent my adult life learning from business owners.

They helped resolve my curiosity when I was a kid wondering where my father was during the days and nights he didn't come home.

I now help business owners work out problems, whether it's getting access to money, fulfilling dreams of business ownership, or creating strategies for growth opportunities.

I get to help people create financial and emotional stability and provide the support I saw my father needed. I want to stop the urge to fulfill our anxiety with vices and worries and reinstate knowledge to properly prepare for the right solutions to problems. A grounded confidence provides us with the emotional foundation and can be developed from something we've always had but lost—curiosity.

Sometimes our anxieties become larger than life, and it can lead to avoidance of people, tasks, and a spiraling loss of confidence. In 2017, The Mindset Project published a message from the president and founder Michael DeVenney, who brings to mind his experiences while battling anxiety and depression throughout his development as a business owner.

"In the drive for start-up and existing companies to achieve economic impact, we are in danger of missing the well-being of the person at the core of the business and vital to its success: the entrepreneur."[116]

---

116 The Mindset Project, "At the Intersection of Entrepreneurship and Positive Mindset Part VI: Entrepreneurial Wellbeing as a Path to Business Success," Accessed August 31, 2020.

The Mindset Project focuses on the emotional challenge of our psychology and showing business owners how to take the initiative to change toward a positive mindset. When we have a positive mindset, we can maximize our positive decisions and opportunities because we work toward grounded confidence and thoughtful actions. This grounded confidence comes from a determined curiosity toward improvement.

Entrepreneurial curiosity is shown to have common elements between entrepreneurs who want to expand their business and improve their business results. They all shared self-efficacy. Per the American Psychology Association, self-efficacy refers to an individual's belief in his or her capacity to execute behaviors necessary to produce specific performance attainments.[117]

In my experience, the most successful business owners always have an entrepreneurial curiosity to learn more about their business and study financial reporting to make reliable decisions and value creation.

I have always been captivated by stories from business owners I get to meet, and I love how unique each one is and how their experiences shape their psyche and decision-making. I love listening to interviews of entrepreneurs who have survived the darkness of business struggles and finally figuring it out and are happy. The late nights, the early mornings,

---

117 A. Bandura, (1977), Self-efficacy: Toward a unifying theory of behavioral change, Psychological Review, 84(2), 191–215. A. Bandura, (1986), Social foundations of thought and action: A social cognitive theory, Englewood Cliffs, NJ: Prentice-Hall. A. Bandura, (1997), Self-Efficacy: The exercise of control, New York, NY: W. H. Freeman.

the ceaseless decisions, revising the work of others, praying money comes in to pay bills—at the core of every business owner is the chance to change their world for the better.

The most common message being advertised is to work harder than your competition mindset, but without the right mix of passion, a strong desire to learn, and financial proficiency, we are destined to fail. The principles of business are being overshadowed by the false sense of security.

I've discovered the obstacles small business owners face are universal, but everyone feels alone when we're going through them. The most common reasons are self-inflicted and created throughout the life of the business and never get addressed properly. With small businesses making up a majority of all US businesses, it is important to address the leading cause of small business closures, which is a lack of *financial education.*

I think it's only right I end with wise words from Warren Buffett. From Berkshire Hathaway's 2020 Annual Letter, "Investing illusions can continue for a surprisingly long time. Wall Street loves the fees that deal-making generates, and the press loves the stories that colorful promoters provide. At a point, also, the soaring price of a promoted stock can itself become the 'proof' that an illusion is reality. Eventually, of course, the party ends, and many business 'emperors' are found to have no clothes. Financial history is replete with the names of famous conglomerates who were initially lionized as business geniuses by journalists, analysts, and investment bankers, but whose creations ended up as business junkyards."[118]

118 Berkshire Hathaway Inc. "2020 Annual Report." Written by Warren E. Buffett, Chairman of the Board., Presented February 27, 2021.

ACKNOWLEDGMENTS

———

I want to thank everyone who was a part of my journey writing *The Curious Business Owner*. There is no way such a blessing would have been realized without the encouragement, prayers, and advice of so many people.

I want to start by thanking my grandma for her selfless love and her tenacious commitment to my education, my mom's guiding words that encouraged me to reach for my dreams, my father's ambition and confident advice that has counseled me along the way. I want to thank my baby sister and brother-in-law for their persistent support of everything I do. To my aunts, uncles, and my entire family, I want you to know I love you guys!

Anyone who knows me knows my best quality is my beautiful, affectionate, diligent wife. There is no one in the world who would sacrifice their life to save mine, except you. Without your strength, I could not live life on my terms, and I can't wait to see what may come. Thank you to my wife's family for their inspiration and faith, and thank you to my father-in-law for modeling what uncompromising faith looks like.

To my kiddos: Jacob, you single-handedly had the biggest impact on my life. As my first baby, you make me aware of my weaknesses and are insightful enough to work with me on building an authentic relationship. Noah, you are my mirror image. I hope to exhibit the lessons I've learned for you. Emma, my little princess, you have weaved me around your tiny finger. You have brought out a tenderness I never knew I was qualified to have.

Thank you to my friends who have always been supportive: Leon Vela and Mary Valenzuela, for investing in my dream to write a book; to Michael Garza, PhD and his wife Amy, for his mentorship and them motivating me to chase my ambitions; to my friends, both business and personal, for the privilege of learning from so many opinions and points of view. Their recommendations, stories, and friendship have helped shape my ideas for this book.

The friends I spoke with gathered their wisdom for the book: Chef Alejandro Barrientos, Michael Crain, Angel Garcia, James Bishop, Daniel Van DerVleet of Cornell University, and business associates Fredda Levario, Erik Barreno, Xavier Gonzales, and Steven Rogers.

Thank you to those who sponsored, enlightened, and supported me during my book's journey:

Adrian Torres	Al Ornelas
Alan Armesto Jr.	Alicia Garza
Alfred Munoz	Andres Robles

Andrew Arriaga

Anna Ulate

Bobby Wright

Brian Schroeder

Carlos Pando

Chikis Anchondo

Dustyn Valencia

Esteban Barrientos

Hector Garcia

Javior Polk

Jerry Valencia

Jessica Cravens

Joe A. Jacobo

Landon Henry

Lori Valencia

Luis Galvan

Manuel Samaniego

Matthew Cravens

Oscar Anchondo

Robert Aguirre

Ron West

Sophia Olivarez

Steve Natividad

Angie Bullard

Blanca Nieto

Brenda Valencia

Carlos Carpizo

Carlos R. Romo

David Bloom

Elie Benavidez

Gilbert Dixon

Jack Pina

Jeffrey Nice

Jesse Ramos

Jill Tucker

Lam Le

Lili & Alfred Carrasco

Louie Ornelas

Manual Castro

Mark Marquez

Monica Lopez

Paul Pallan

Roman Alvarez

Rya Stone

Steve Dowling

The Vuelvas Family

I must thank the team at New Degree Press for their hard work and for supporting me during my publishing journey, including David Grandouiller and Cynthia Tucker, who coached me through the process and made sure I stayed aligned with my publishing dreams. Thank you to John Saunders, who encouraged me throughout my publishing campaign, and Linda Berardelli, who kept me updated and on schedule.

I especially need to thank Eric Koester from the Creator Institute and Georgetown University for his encouragement and coaching. Without your phone call on a random afternoon, I wouldn't have accomplished one of the hardest things I've ever done and found my new passion, writing.

APPENDIX

INTRODUCTION

BuffettMungerWisdom. "The Psychology of Human Misjudgment—Charlie Munger Full Speech." January 13, 2013. Video, 2:04. https://youtu.be/pqzcCfUglws

Elkins, Kathleen. "Berkshire Hathaway star followed Warren Buffett's advice: Read 500 pages a day." MSNBC, March 27, 2018. accessed February 27, 2021. https://www.cnbc.com/2018/03/27/warren-buffetts-key-tip-for-success-read-500-pages-a-day.html.

Kashdan, Todd B., Paul Rose, and Frank D. Fincham. "Curiosity and exploration: Facilitating positive subjective experiences and personal growth opportunities." Journal of personality assessment 82, no. 3 (2004): 291–305.

Le Cunff, Anne-Laure. "The science of curiosity: why we keep asking 'why.'" https://nesslabs.com/science-of-curiosity

Sanders, Tim. "Put your network to good use." Tim Sanders Blog. June 9, 2009. accessed December 12, 2020. https://timsanders. com/put-your-network-to-good-use/.

"Staying Curious." Investment Masters Class." (Investment blog). June 28, 2018. accessed October 22, 2020. http://mastersinvest. com/newblog/2018/5/19/curiosity.

Strömbäck, Camilla, Thérèse Lind, Kenny Skagerlund, Daniel Västfjäll, and Gustav Tinghög. "Does self-control predict financial behavior and financial well-being?" Journal of Behavioral and Experimental Finance 14 (2017): 30–38.

CHAPTER ONE: BE CURIOUS

Alternative Education Center. "Mission/vision." https://www. ectorcountyisd.org/domain/9. accessed January 13, 2021.

Dahmen, Pearl, and Eileen Rodríguez. "Financial Literacy and the Success of Small Businesses: An Observation from a Small Business Development Center." Numeracy: Advancing Education in Quantitative Literacy 7, no. 1 (2014).

Lanning, Kimber. "Lack of Access to Capital is Crippling the US Small Business Sector in Communities of Color." Interise. https://interise.org/lack-of-access-to-capital-is-crippling-the- us-small-business-sector-in-communities-of-color/.

Miller, Holly Ventura, J. C. Barnes, and Kevin M. Beaver. "Self-con- trol and health outcomes in a nationally representative sample." American journal of health behavior 35, no. 1 (2011): 15–27.

Panko, Riley. "Why Small Businesses Lack Accounting Resources in 2018." Clutch Report (blog). Clutch. October 1, 2018. https://clutch.co/accounting/resources/why-small-businesses-lack-accounting-resources-2018.

Strömbäck, Camilla, Thérèse Lind, Kenny Skagerlund, Daniel Västfjäll, and Gustav Tinghög. "Does self-control predict financial behavior and financial well-being?" *Journal of Behavioral and Experimental Finance* 14 (2017): 30–38.

Ucbasaran, Deniz, Dean A. Shepherd, Andy Lockett, and S. John Lyon. "Life after business failure: The process and consequences of business failure for entrepreneurs." *Journal of management* 39, no. 1 (2013): 163–202.

"What is Ratio Analysis?" Investopedia. accessed January 10, 2021.

CHAPTER TWO: STAY CURIOUS

Adomako, S. and Danso, A. "Financial Literacy and Firm performance: The moderating role of financial capital availability and resource flexibility." International Journal of Management & Organizational Studies, 3 (4). (2014).

Burke, E. "A philosophical enquiry into the origin of our ideas of the sublime and beautiful." London. Routledge & Kegan Paul. (1958. Original work published 1757).

Campion, M. A., & Lord, R. G. "A control systems conceptualization of the goal setting and changing process." Organizational Behavior and Human Performance, 30, 265–287. (1982).

Dawkins, R. Unweaving the rainbow: science, delusion and the appetite for wonder. New York: Teachers College Press. (1998).

Day, H.I. "Curiosity and the interested explorer." Performance and Instruction. 21. 19–22.

Egan, K., Cant, A., & Judson, G. *Wonder-full education: the centrality of wonder in teaching and learning across the curriculum.* New York: Routledge. (2014).

Encyclopedia of Children's Health. "Cognitive Development." accessed May 7, 2021. http://www.healthofchildren.com/C/Cognitive-Development.html.

Gino, Francesca. "The business case for curiosity." *Harvard Business Review* 96, no. 5 (2018): 48–57.

"Intangible Asset." Investopedia. https://www.investopedia.com/terms/i/intangibleasset.asp, accessed February 27, 2021.

"39 Entrepreneur Statistics You Need to Know in 2021." Smallbiz Genius. accessed March 1, 2021.

Koestler, A. "The act of creation." New York: Dell. (1973).; Simon, H. "The cat that curiosity couldn't kill." Working paper. Department of Psychology. Carnegie Mellon University. (1992).

Koo, M., & Fishbach, A. (2008). Dynamics of self-regulation: How (un)accomplished goal actions affect motivation. Journal of Personality and Social Psychology, 94(2), 183–195.

Lev, Baruch. "The deteriorating usefulness of financial report information and how to reverse it, Accounting and Business Research." 48:5, 465–493, DOI:10.1080/00014788.2018.147013 8. (2018).

Lindholm, Markus. "Promoting curiosity?" *Science & Education* 27, no. 9–10 (2018): 987–1002.

Locke, E. A., & Baum, J. "Entrepreneurial motivation." In J. Baum, M. Frese, & R. A. Baron (Eds.). *The psychology of entrepreneurship* (pp. 93–112). Mahwah: Lawrence Erlbaum Associates. (2007).

Merriam-Webster. s.v. "intangible *(adj.)*." accessed January 6, 2021.

Opdal, P. M. Curiosity, wonder and education seen as perspective development. Studies in Philosophy and Education. 20, 331–344. (2001).

Rauch, A., & Frese, M. "Born to be an entrepreneur?" Revising the personality approach to entrepreneurship. In J. R. Baum, M. Frese, & R. A. Baron (Eds.). The psychology of entrepreneurship (pp. 41–65). Mahwah: Erlbaum. (2007).

"Reading the Balance Sheet." Investopedia. accessed February 27, 2021. https://www.investopedia.com/articles/04/031004.asp.

Russell Sarder, "What is the main reason standard accounting principles are not useful?" December 11, 2018, video, :35 https://www.youtube.com/watch?v=I8NG-y9hdEU, accessed January 23, 2021.

Scott, Mel, Richard Bruce. "Five stages of growth in small business." Long Range Planning, Volume 20, Issue 3, 1987, Pages 45–52, ISSN 0024-6301, https://doi.org/10.1016/0024-6301(87)90071-9, (https://www.sciencedirect.com/science/article/pii/0024630187900719)

Stern, D.N. "The interpersonal world of the child." New York: Basic Books. (2007).

Stokoe, Robert. "Curiosity, a condition for learning." The International Schools Journal 32, no. 1 (2012): 63.

"The Gap Between Large and Small Companies Is Growing. Why.?" Harvard Business Review. accessed January 14, 2021. https://hbr.org/2019/08/the-gap-between-large-and-small-companies-is-growing-why.

The Coca-Cola Company. "Warren Buffett on Why He'll Never Sell a Share of Coke Stock." Coca-Cola 2013 Annual Shareowners meeting. YouTube video,:48. https://youtu.be/4p1_5bZ8I4M.

"The unbalanced balance sheet: Making intangibles count." PricewaterhouseCoopers. accessed February 24, 2021. https://viewpoint.pwc.com/dt/us/en/pwc/points_of_view/assets/povmarketcapvsbook.pdf.

"Top 6 Reasons New Businesses Fail." Investopedia. accessed January 23, 2021.

Ucbasaran, Deniz & Shepherd, Dean & Lockett, Andy & Lyon, John. "Life After Business Failure: The Process and Consequences *of Business Failure for Entrepreneurs.*" Journal of Management. 39. 163 2002. 10.1177/0149206312457823. (2013).

Wofford, J. C., Goodwin, V. L., & Premack, S. "Meta-analysis of the antecedents of personal goal level and of the antecedents and consequences of goal commitment." *Journal of Management,* 18, 595–615. (1992).

CHAPTER THREE: FUTURE BELONGS TO THE CURIOUS

"Becoming Warren Buffett," directed by Peter W. Kunhardt, written by Chris Chuang, release date January 30, 2017.

Binson, Bussakorn. "Curiosity-Based Learning (CBL) Program." *Online Submission* 6, no. 12 (2009): 13–22.

Canterucci, J. Personal brilliance: Mastering the everyday habits that create a lifetime of success. New York: AMACOM Books. (2005).

Jeraj, Mitja & Antončič, B. "A Conceptualization of Entrepreneurial Curiosity and Construct Development: A Multi-Country Empirical Validation." *Creativity Research Journal.* 25(4), 426–435. http://dx.doi.org/10.1 080/10400419.2013.843350. (2013).

Jeraj, Mitja & Maric, Miha. "Entrepreneurial Curiosity—The New Construct." *High potentials, lean organization, internet of things: proceedings of the 32nd International Conference on Organizational Science Development.* (str. 289–298). Kranj: Moderna organizacija. (2013b).

Kang MJ, et al. The Wick in the Candle of Learning: Epistemic Curiosity Activates Reward Circuitry and Enhances Memory. Psychological Science. 2009;20(8):963-973. doi:10.1111/j.1467-9280.2009.02402.x

Loewenstein, George. "The psychology of curiosity: A review and reinterpretation." *Psychological Bulletin* 116, no. 1 (1994): 75.

Mueller, Stephen L., and Anisya S. Thomas. "Culture and entrepreneurial potential: A nine country study of locus of control and innovativeness." *Journal of Business Venturing* 16, no. 1 (2001): 51–75.

Scott, Mel and Bruce, Richard, "Five Stages of Growth in Small Business," Long Range Planning 20, no. 3, 45–52.

The Mindset Project. "At the Intersection of Entrepreneurship and Positive Mindset Part VI: Entrepreneurial Wellbeing as a Path to Business Success." Accessed August 31, 2020.

Peljko, Ziga, Mitja Jeraj, Gheorghe Săvoiu, and Miha Marič. "An empirical study of the relationship between entrepreneurial curiosity and innovativeness." Organizacija 49, no. 3 (2016).

CHAPTER FOUR: CONFIDENCE AND CURIOSITY

Brown, Brené. *Dare to Lead: Brave Work. Tough Conversations. Whole Hearts.* Random House, 2018.

Buheji, Mohamed. "Designing a Curious Life." AuthorHouse, UK (2019).

Buheji, Mohamed. "Optimising the 'Economics of Curiosity' for Better Future Foresight." (2020): 21–28.

Bougie, Nicolas, and Ryutaro Ichise. "Skill-based curiosity for intrinsically motivated reinforcement learning." *Machine Learning* 109, no. 3 (2020): 493–512.

Gage, Deborah. "The venture capital secret: 3 out of 4 start-ups fail." *Wall Street Journal* 20 (2012).

Kashdan, Todd B., Paul Rose, and Frank D. Fincham. "Curiosity and exploration: Facilitating positive subjective experiences and personal growth opportunities." *Journal of personality assessment* 82, no. 3 (2004): 291–305.

Loewenstein, George (1994). "The psychology of curiosity: a review and reinterpretation." *Psychological Bulletin, 116* (1), 75–98.

Salovey, Peter, and John D. Mayer. "Emotional intelligence." *Imagination, cognition and personality* 9, no. 3 (1990): 185–211.

Van Velsor, Ellen, Patricia Hind, Andrew Wilson, and Gilbert Lenssen. "Developing leaders for sustainable business." *Corporate Governance: The international journal of business in society* (2009).

CHAPTER SIX: CURIOSITY IS THE ENGINE OF ACHIEVEMENT

Buheji, Mohamed. "Optimising the 'Economics of Curiosity' for Better Future Foresight." (2020): 21–28.

Eby, L. T., & McManus, S. E. (2004). "The protege's role in negative mentoring experiences." Journal of Vocational Behavior, 65, 255–275.

Leedham, Melville. "The coaching scorecard: A holistic approach to evaluating the benefits of business coaching." PhD diss., Oxford Brookes University, 2004.

Schermuly, Carsten C., and Carolin Graßmann. "A literature review on negative effects of coaching—what we know and what we need to know." Coaching: An International Journal of Theory, Research and Practice 12, no. 1 (2019): 39–66.

Wisdomfuel. "Cardone University Review—Is Grant Cardone Legit?." accessed October 4, 2021. https://wisdomfuel.com/grant-cardone-university-review/.

CHAPTER SEVEN: CURIOSITY TAKES IGNORANCE SERIOUSLY

Buffett, Mary and David Clark, *Warren Buffett and the Interpretation of Financial Statements: The Search for the Company with a Durable Competitive Advantage*. Read by Karen White. Tantor Audio, December 1, 2008.

Schermuly, Carsten C., and Carolin Graßmann. "A literature review on negative effects of coaching—what we know and what we need to know." *Coaching: An International Journal of Theory, Research and Practice* 12, no. 1 (2019): 39–66.

CHAPTER EIGHT: CURIOSITY IS THE MOST IMPORTANT PART

Benjamin, James J., and Arthur J. Francia and Robert H. Strawser, Financial Accounting, (2015), page number.

Bozer, G., & Jones, R. J. "Understanding the factors that determine workplace coaching effectiveness: A systematic literature review." European Journal of Work and Organizational Psychology. 27(3), 342–361. doi:10.1080/1359432X.2018.1446946. (2018).

Theeboom, T., Beersma, B., & van Vianen, A. E. M. "Does coaching work? A meta-analysis on the effects of coaching on individual level outcomes in an organizational context." The Journal of Positive Psychology, 9, 1–18. doi:10.1080/17439760.2013.837499. (2014).

Wong, Alexandra, Scott Holmes, and Michael T. Schaper. "How do small business owners actually make their financial decisions? Understanding SME financial behaviour using a case-based approach." Small Enterprise Research 25, no. 1 (2018): 36–51.

Sadowski, Jathan. "When data is capital: Datafication, accumulation, and extraction." Big Data & Society 6, no. 1 (2019): 2053951718820549.

CHAPTER NINE: INTANGIBLE IS THE SEED OF THE TANGIBLE

Andrews, K. (1965). The concept of corporate strategy. Homewood, IL: Dow Jones–Irwin.

Becker, B. E., & Huselid, M. A. "Strategic human resource management: Where do we go from here?" Journal of Management.32, 898–925. (2006).doi:10.1177/0149206306293668.

Bowen, D. E., & Ostroff, C. "Understanding HRM firm performance linkages: The role of "strength" of the HRM system." Academy of Management Review. 29, 203–221. (2004). doi:10.2307/20159029.

Chandler, A. D. (1962). Strategy and structure: Chapters in the history of American industrial enterprise. London, England: MIT Press.

Combs, J., Liu, Y., Hall, A., & Ketchen, D. (2006). "How much do high-performance work practices matter? A meta-analysis of their effects on organizational performance." Personnel Psychology, 59, 501–528. doi:10.1111/j.1744-6570.2006.00045.x.

Elkins, Kathleen. "Berkshire Hathaway star followed Warren Buffett's advice: Read 500 pages a day." Makeit(blog). March 27, 2018. https://www.cnbc.com/2018/03/27/warren-buffetts-key-tip-for-success-read-500-pages-a-day.html.

Hambrick, D. C., & Mason, P. A. (1984). "Upper echelons: The organization as a reflection of its top managers." Academy of Management Review, 9, 193–206. doi:10.2307/258434.

Huselid, M. A. "The impact of human resource management practices on turnover, productivity, and corporate financial performance." Academy of Management Journal. 38, 635–672. (1995). doi:10.2307/256741

Kaplan, Robert S., and David P. Norton. "Measuring the strategic readiness of intangible assets." Harvard business review 82, no. 2 (2004): 52–63.

Kidd, Celeste, and Benjamin Y. Hayden. "The psychology and neuroscience of curiosity." Neuron 88, no. 3 (2015): 449–460.

Kor, Y., & Mahoney, J. T. (2005). "How dynamics, management, and governance of resource deployments influence firm-level performance." Strategic Management Journal, 26, 489–496. doi:10.1002/smj.459

Le, H., Oh, I. S., Shaffer, J., & Schmidt, F. Implications of methodological advances for the practice of personnel selection: How practitioners benefit from meta-analysis. Academy of Management Perspectives. (2007). 21, 6–15.

Luthans F. 2002b. Positive organizational behavior: Developing and managing psychological strengths. Acad. Manag. Exec. 16(1):57–72.

Luthans, Fred, and Carolyn M. Youssef-Morgan. "Psychological capital: An evidence-based positive approach." Annual review of organizational psychology and organizational behavior 4 (2017): 339–366.

Sadowski, Jathan. "When data is capital: Datafication, accumulation, and extraction." Big Data & Society 6, no. 1 (2019): 2053951718820549.

Seligman MEP. 1998. Learned Optimism. New York: Pocket Books.

Snyder CR, Irving L, Anderson J. 1991. Hope and health: Measuring the will and the ways. In Handbook of Social and Clinical Psychology, ed. CR Snyder, DR Forsyth, pp. 285–305. Elmsford, NY: Pergamon.

Stajkovic AD, Luthans F. 1998b. Social cognitive theory and self-efficacy: Going beyond traditional motivational and behavioral approaches. Organ. Dyn. 26:62–74.

"Staying Curious," Investment Masters Class," (Investment Blog), June 28, 2018, accessed October 22, 2020. http://mastersinvest.com/newblog/2018/5/19/curiosity.

Subramony, M., Krause, N., Norton, J., & Burns, G. N. The relationship between human resource investments and organizational performance: A firm-level examination of equilibrium theory. Journal of Applied Psychology. 93, (2008). 778–788. doi:10.1037/0021-9010.93.4.778.

The Coca-Cola Company. "Warren Buffett on Why He'll Never Sell a Share of Coke Stock." Coca-Cola 2013 Annual Shareowners meeting. YouTube video, :48. https://youtu.be/4p1_5bZ8I4M.

Vigeant, Margot A., M. Prince, K. Nottis, and A. Golightly. "Curious about student curiosity: Implications of pedagogical approach for students' mindset." Proceedings of American Association for Engineering Education (2018).

CHAPTER TEN: THE VALUE OF CURIOSITY IS TO USE IT

Engel, S. The case for curiosity. Educational Leadership, 70(5):3640, 2013.

CONCLUSION

Berkshire Hathaway Inc. "2020 Annual Report." Written by Warren E. Buffett, Chairman of the Board., Presented February 27,
2021. https://www.berkshirehathaway.com/2020ar/2020ar.pdf.

The Mindset Project. "At the Intersection of Entrepreneurship and
Positive Mindset Part VI: Entrepreneurial Wellbeing as a Path
to Business Success." Accessed August 31, 2020.

Bandura, A. 1977. "Self-efficacy: Toward a unifying theory of
behavioral change." Psychological Review, 84(2), 191–215. Bandura, A.1986. "Social foundations of thought and action: A
social cognitive theory." Englewood Cliffs. NJ: Prentice-Hall.
Bandura, A. 1997. "Self-Efficacy: The exercise of control." New
York, NY: W. H. Freeman.

Made in the USA
Middletown, DE
25 September 2022

10912234R00106